Rent to Own Your First Home

Squall Publishing
Seattle, Washington

Rent to Own Your First Home: An American Dream Story

by John Boyle

Printed in the United States of America

First Printing, 2014

ISBN 978-0-9833966-4-2
Squall Publishing
squallpublishing.com

www.rent2ownbook.com
Cover image: siuwing | 123RF stock photo

for Allison

ACKNOWLEDGEMENTS

Many thanks to Jack Boyle, Jennifer Boyle, Kathleen Boyle, Hugh McEntire, Susan Williams, Nathaniel Williams, Michael Press, Dr. Grant Thrall and most importantly to my love, wife, and partner in all of the difficult things that make life worth getting out of bed for in the morning, Allison McEntire.

TABLE OF CONTENTS

1. Introduction   11
2. Challenges   17
3. Saving Money   33
4. Credit   45
5. Plan B   70
6. Be Happy   78
7. Finding a Rent-to-Own Home   104
8. Found a House!   126
9. Asking for Help   146
10. Raising Money   157
11. For Sellers   175
12. Finding the American Dream   193

"A man is like a novel: until the very last
page you do not know how it will end.
Otherwise it would not be worth reading."

Yevgeny Zamyatin

INTRODUCTION

Some stories work well when you get to the ending first.
Our story, my wife Allison and mine, is so much fun to
tell when I start with the ending that I am going to start
with the good times. We ended where we began, searching on Zillow.com. Zillow is a Seattle-based real estate
marketplace that does a great job empowering real estate
consumers and agents with accurate and up-to-date real
estate market data. We decided to revisit Zillow after we
officially closed on our home to see an estimation of what
happened to its value since we first discovered it. (It took
a few days to getting around to this because we did not do
much in the first days after we closed. It was as if we both
carried this heavy burden on our shoulders for years and
once we closed we could finally relax.) This time when we
looked our home up on Zillow.com it showed our property's estimated value at $365,000. The loan that we just
signed had a remaining balance of $206,000.

That meant that on the day we closed we made,
according to Zillow's estimate, $149,000 in equity. Making
almost $150,000 in a day seemed like some other person's

11

life, and I have to admit that it was an awesome feeling to know we did it.

Our journey ended with the happiest ending: our best case scenario came true. Was it luck? Luck always plays some part in success, but when you read our story you will see that we put ourselves in a position to get the deal done by working hard enough to get important help from other hard workers... with a little luck thrown in as well.

As I mentioned, when we started looking for a potential rent-to-own home we started our search with Zillow.com, and they were not as kind to our home when we first discovered the listing in early 2012. In reality they were doing their typically great job at providing accurate real estate data and it was bleak everywhere, even in West Seattle. It showed our eventual home's value had been in steep decline for some months and that it was currently in danger of foreclosure. It said "rent-to-own" in the description. It was pretty obvious that whoever wrote that description was prepared to quickly rent their home out with an intent to sell it. It was exactly where we wanted to live, and it was exactly what we were looking for. We decided to go for it.

We were warned. Lots of well-meaning friends and family warned us against going the rent-to-own route. They informed us that the housing market was still too volatile. They told us that "rent-to-own" is typically a scam, or that rent-to-own contracts take advantage of those with poor credit. They also told us of the stats for rent-to-own home contracts: more than 50% fail, and again they were correct. None of this was news to us, as we also found this information when we researched our options.

So why did we ignore all of this seemingly good advice and research? Because 50% DON'T fail. Because we found one key component missing from the rent-to-own equation: resources from those who succeeded in purchasing their rent-to-own home. Because there had to be more to the picture than doom and gloom. We vowed that if we got our home via a rent-to-own, we were going to create a resource to help fill the void of "how to's" from those who have actually purchased a rent-to-own home.

Rent-to-own success stories are out there. Since telling our story I have met other home owners who have purchased their home through a rent-to-own, or as they are officially called "a lease option," and most of them also made great investments in their futures. Upon meeting our neighbor across the street and explaining our situation, we found that he too used a lease option to purchase his home many years earlier. There have also been a number of helpful new books written about rent-to-own home purchasing. This is an avenue to home ownership that seems to be gaining a lot of traction in recent months, but the landscape was still empty of resources with first-hand experience until now.

Why don't we hear from more buyers? Successful buyers seem to be more occupied with their new home, and why not? In some circles there is a negative stigma attached to the words "rent-to-own" so leaving that out of the story might actually make it a better one for people to share. Couple that potential stigma with the fact that at the end of most lease option agreements the process of obtaining a home loan from the bank can be exactly the same as for other purchases, so it can feel like the more traditional approach to home ownership. These factors likely contribute to the void of first-hand accounts of successful lease option purchases.

Imagine for a minute what a potential home buyer feels who fails to close the lease option deal on their rental home. They will have invested lots of money and time in their credit, savings, home, and neighborhood only to have a bank tell them they still do not qualify for a loan in time to close the deal. If they must walk away they lose thousands of dollars from their option payment and the dream home they have been making life plans in for the past few years. Relationships at schools, churches and community groups become severed or lost. They have to return to the days of apartment hunting and preparing for expensive and difficult moves. It might end up setting them back years on their goal of home ownership or cause them to abandon it for good as expenses pile up when they have to make a sudden move.

Renters in those situations are likely to be hurt

and upset. I do not blame them. Because of this, they are more likely to tell their stories to warn others and those painful stories are more likely to stick and be repeated in the general conversations that people associate with attempts to purchase a rent-to-own home. Remember that this general scenario represents the way most people believe rent-to-own home agreements will end up. We know many others who, like us, know they can afford a home, are ready to stop throwing their hard earned money away on rent, and want to make a sound life investment even though they seem invisible to the banks. We want your experience to be a lot more like ours than the other 50 percent, which is why I feel it is so important for us to share how we found and purchased our home.

I think that our story can help others cut the guess work out of making so many of the hard decisions faced during the rent-to-own journey. You can try to replicate how we did it, and depending on where you live or if you are willing to relocate, you could do it. We recognize some housing markets are still in deep recession and there are still people being kicked out of homes and others under water to the point at which it feels better to take the loss. Because of this our story might sound impossible, and making $149,000 in equity on the first day you own your home is hardly the norm, but consider that had we gone the normal route we would have most likely gotten the normal first-time buyers' result. If you are still having trouble believing it's possible, keep reading because our story gets even more improbable.

Back in April of 2012 on the day we signed the agreement to purchase our home for $212,700, my credit score was 585 and Allison's was just 600. That is correct. While we had already begun the rehabilitation process, our credit was still very bad; we walked away with a signed lease option contract to purchase a $212,700 home with an average credit score of under 600. Just weeks earlier we were laughed out of a mortgage broker's office. It was very clear he did not take us seriously, and I felt ready to prove him wrong. If you are like us, steadily employed and ready to work hard and willing to stick it out no matter the odds, you too can write your own rent-to-own home success story. Over the next eleven chapters I will lead you through exactly how we did it and give you the advice we wish we had when we started.

Following the "how to" chapters we will examine all of the factors that came into play for this unique result to happen. In the end writing and telling our story was humbling. I realized that we were fortunate to live a modern American dream story that would not have been possible without so many others pursuing their own American dream just like us.

"When there is no enemy
within, the enemy outside
cannot hurt you."

Winston Churchill

CHALLENGES

Before I get into the story of how we found and bought our home, it is important to start this book with the most difficult opposition that I faced throughout the entire 27 month marathon purchase: me. There were plenty of people who I trust who advised me against trying a rent-to-own agreement. You too may have your head filled with all kinds of ideas as to why you cannot or should not try to rentto-own a home. There were many times when I wanted to give up. Something was telling me that it is just too hard or even impossible. I saw friends and family follow conventional paths to home ownership, and it looked so much easier for them. My brain added to that feeling all of the advice from those who felt it was too risky. Even though they have no experience trying a rent-to-own situation, they genuinely believed they were giving me the best possible advice. There were plenty of times that giving up or quitting or settling for a life that was less than what I wanted seemed like the reasonable thing to do. It was not and is not reasonable at all! Why settle for less than you believe you can achieve? It is bad enough when other people try to define you as less than what you know you are worth. If you live under that expectation, then you make it your reality. Only you can make your reality, so why not make it the reality you want?

Trust me, tough times and self doubt will likely happen to you too if you try a lease option home purchase. It is much easier for me to write this advice with the benefit of hindsight than it was for me to believe before I achieved my goal. I knew that I had to be confident in my knowledge of cities and real estate markets, and I was. I knew I had to use that information and perspective to lesson the risk and increase the reward, and I did. I never doubted that I could do it. Even when people said, "you should not do it" I understood that they lacked my education and experience with real estate market data and therefore lacked the bigger picture.

Understand that people mean well when they tell you not to try. They simply think that normal and conventional is common because it is safe, and safe advice is good advice. In the case of our rent-to-own purchase they were not giving the best possible advice. Had we shied away from the risks associated with a rent-to-own agreement, and waited until we were "ready" for the conventional path, we would have been priced out of Seattle as home buying has become competitive and the market here is red-hot. I know where I am happiest and it would have been devastating to sacrifice living in Seattle, a compromise I was not willing to make.

There is old audio footage of me on a radio interview back in 1994 explaining what I knew about Seattle. When the DJ asked me how I knew so much about the city I let him know that one day I was going to live there. I have wanted to live here since I was 17 years old, and had I listened to the "safe" advice I would have missed the first and potentially only opportunity for me to own a home in the city I love. It would have also been devastating to pass by what is now our home and wonder if we could have achieved it. Especially considering we could have been wondering that from an apartment, still paying rent to fund someone else's Seattle dream home.

The "safe" path to home ownership would have meant sacrificing a higher level of happiness. When others were using the word "safe" in their advice to us they meant preventing risk of financial loss. They made the mistake of thinking of "safe" in terms of money and not in terms of happiness. For some reason in my life I have not ever confused money with happiness. Perhaps that comes from my humble beginnings, but happiness has always brought more value to my life than money. In our case what made us happiest turned out to be a much safer financial outcome for us and our future anyway. I have found that seems to be the way that it works for me. Work hard for happiness and money and the financial security it provides will follow.

The current against us felt strong at times, making the journey feel impossible, but we continued forward with our plan anyway. As we did, our goal became less dreamy and more real, and a much better looking investment. As that happened more and more people actually started to support us.

It became contagious. The more we stuck it out and worked hard, the more people saw our progress and wanted to help. They started to see the potential in our deal and they soon began rooting for us. We went from silly dreamers to a couple sitting on the investment of a lifetime.

People find confidence attractive. If you plan well enough and work hard enough, you will gain the confidence in yourself to attract the support from others that you will need to close the deal, and believe me you will need support. Optimism, tenacity and passion have to outweigh any fear, doubt, stress and everyday aches and pains. If you find the strength to maintain those qualities over years, those who tried to talk you out of trying your deal will be helping you achieve your goal in the end.

What this taught us was that we are completely capable of creating our own reality, and if we could do it with our situation believe me, you can too. But we did not do it alone. There were a lot of people who were necessary to help us create the reality of home ownership. That is okay. In fact, it is how it should be. We all need each other. There was actually a lot of safety in knowing that we needed help with our biggest goal. If we needed help that means that there is help out there and through knowing that, we went out and found it.

Believe in yourself; it is a part of being confident anyway. You can achieve big goals that you set for yourself because others will begin to believe in you as well. This is important because you can easily talk yourself out of trying to get a home or even out of closing the deal. It sounds silly but, just like us, most of the time you will likely be your own biggest obstacle... even though by doing so you are working against your own dreams and aspirations and even though talking yourself out of trying to own a home can prevent yourself from being able to pass wealth down through your family. Knowing all of this and knowing that it can help to stabilize your family's life, you will try to talk yourself out of even trying. Why will you do this? For the very same reason I almost did: fear.

I doubted we could do it many times when I became afraid of something that had to do with our home. I would find myself thinking about what failure would look like and soon I would start believing we would fail. When self doubt would become part of my vision I would remember to focus on the upside instead. I would also remember to tell myself that self doubt exists in all people. Some people can ignore it and stay focused on their goals regardless; others allow fear of coming up short to prevent them from even trying to see if they can do it.

You will certainly doubt that you can do it as you move forward, and so will a lot of other people around you. Make it your mission to prove them wrong, and more importantly to prove to yourself that you can achieve your goals. Imagine inviting them to your house-warming party. You can do it. Some of you reading this book right now will take a seemingly impossible situation and turn it into a realized dream of home ownership just like Allison and I did. I hope that is you.

The best example I can give you is how self destructive I was to our goal in the spring of 2014. I was working a demanding full-time job, starting a business, writing this book, working on fixer-upper house projects, and splitting time playing lease-option real estate agent with Allison. I was completely exhausted. The demands of those projects were weighing on me for over a year, and after 12 to 14 months of many remaining a "project" (improving daily but still far from completion) I decided that something had to give. I typically held myself to an extremely high standard at my job. I did not measure myself against my peers, but rather against big goals that I would set for myself and go after with utter tenacity. With so much on my plate I suddenly found myself doing the bare minimum at work. Others, used to the high standard of work I set for myself, recognized that something was wrong.

The problem was what I was seeing was far worse than what they were seeing. Not only was I becoming average at my job, suddenly that "just do the minimum" attitude necessary for me to survive each day was pouring over into my other projects. Suddenly I was becoming average.

One Sunday as the creeping dread of Monday grew and grew, I decided to quit my job. The embarrassment of showing up average every day after operating at such a high level for so many years was killing me. I started getting called into 1-on-1's where others seemed to assume I didn't care or was growing lazy. Quitting made the most sense as I could focus on our business and work tirelessly to get that up off the ground. We had a plan and plenty of runway to get it going, but quitting my job also would have meant giving up on buying our rent-to-own home. Why would we have to give up our house? Because banks want to see 24 months of steady employment at one employer with a high enough income to show that I could afford to make the monthly mortgage payments. Quitting would have meant at the very least another two years before we could get financed which would have meant the deal for our home was likely dead.

I sent my resignation to our Executive Vice President and let go of my dream of home ownership for the foreseeable future knowing that we would find a way to get there down the road.

My employer apparently knew something was wrong and set up a series of meetings with me and with layers of management. I explained in detail everything that was going on in my life and they offered to support me as I worked through it. I could not believe it. They offered to give me a break where I could use the copious amounts of leave time I had banked to continue to get paid and eventually come back to work when my leave ended. This meant that I could still close on our home and show the bank that I was still steadily employed and receiving a paycheck. It worked, and we closed the deal just two weeks later. That is correct; we closed the deal just two weeks after I almost quit my job.

I had no idea we were only two weeks away at that point because for a couple of weeks there was not communication from our bank, and up until that point we had failed to close the deal five times over six months, so it felt like a holding pattern of disappointment.

We did not get word back from the bank that everything was moving so quickly towards closing this time because our loan officer was out on vacation. If I would have quit then we would have missed this investment by just over two weeks because Michael Press, an extremely hard worker and our loan officer, was taking a much needed and well deserved break. Am I lucky that I had a good employer? You bet. If not I would have found a surefire way to defeat myself and my dream of owning a home in Seattle.

Seth Godin, in his book *The Dip*, outlines this

self-defeating moment very well. He explains that "The Dip" is that difficult point at which most people quit on their goal even though they are just about to achieve it. Like so many others I came right up to the point of letting the dip defeat me. Now that I have lived through a dip and discovered Godin's book, I am prepared for the dips I will face moving forward in my life, but it does not mean that it will be any less difficult to navigate and get through those dips. Godin points out that not only is the dip the most difficult point on your journey to achieving your goal, it is also being able to do all of the most difficult things that it takes to be great at something. In our case this meant working hard to create a successful rent-to-own plan, with no point of reference, and working as hard as we could to keep it on track to close the deal like professional agents (which we are not).

Nearly quitting my job days before we closed on the biggest investment of our lives is the biggest example of how I was my own worst enemy, or maybe even "THE dip", but it is not the only example I could give you. It happens to represent the most difficult time when most people give up, quit or fail, so I felt that it was the most important example to share. You can learn from my biggest mistake, and I hope you do.

It is also fair to say that in looking back over the total experience, even going back to the months leading up to our search when we were researching just how rent-to-own deals worked, the majority of our decisions were good ones. I am proud of how hard we worked and how well we planned, but no plan is perfect and neither am I, so things definitely went wrong. It is the self-defeating things that made it so difficult and those are what you want to avoid.

With that said you should always be on the look out for self-defeating thoughts, advice, attitudes, moods, actions, and other challenges. One good way to make sure you can keep yourself on track is by asking yourself before making every decision, "does this move me closer to closing on my home loan?" Very simple, but if you remember that you are simultaneously your own hero and villain you give yourself a chance to make the heroic decision each time. Will you make some bad choices? No doubt. No one is perfect, but the cumulative effect of keeping yourself focused on your goal will be a powerful force in getting you there in the end, and you will look back on those bad choices and laugh (or cringe, and then laugh).

In the spring of 2013, right in the middle of our rent-to-own purchase I stumbled upon Olivia Fox's incredible book, The Charisma Myth. Fox outlines how anyone can have true power-engaging charisma, and why it is a myth that some people are just born with it. While having charisma is certainly helpful for closing your rent-to-own deal, what her book taught me that was most important to closing on our home was about how our brains work and how they interpret fear and instinct in our everyday experiences and interactions, including all of the important decisions we had to make to reach our goal. This was an important perspective for me as we entered into the very difficult stretch in which we had to close on a home in a red-hot market with shaky credit. Negative thoughts entered into my everyday experience time and time again. Reading Fox's book prepared me for how to deal with those thoughts by allowing me to understand that the feelings that went with them were simply all in my head. I was able to keep that perspective and stay positive and focused even when we were so close to closing the deal yet being rejected by the bank time and time again. As I mentioned before, even with Fox's powerful perspective I still almost ended the deal anyway. It was that hard. Do not underestimate how hard it will be to close on your rent-to-own home. This is why you have to work hard to not allow those self-defeating thoughts to win.

Here is another way of looking at it: Being one's own worst enemy is a way of saying that you will need help to reach your goal, but you will not need any help to fail. You alone can single-handedly end your journey to home ownership any time you want. Just call the home owners and tell them you are moving out. There, done deal. They keep the option money and you go rent an apartment. However you alone cannot magically make it happen and easily close the deal. There are a lot of hard working people out there who want to help you achieve your goals. In many cases it is their job to do so, and in many cases you will absolutely need their help. You have to be able to match their hard work and effort and they will take notice of you and your goals. In our case we had to work hard at making a rent-to-own work, and eventually someone noticed that we were working hard to make a great investment. Had we not matched their work ethic or just given up they would have thought that it was all too good to be true and stayed away from working with us.

One way to begin to help you avoid working against yourself is to be proactive. Simply start taking action to move yourself forward right now as you read this. You will need a lot of documentation in order to close a mortgage with a bank. They will want to see pay stubs, W-2's, documentation of any additional taxable assets, receipts for all months' rent paid toward your lease option, letters explaining any negative marks on your credit, all records of bills paid at the property, and all your receipts for any work that you do or for any contractors you must hire.

You also have to make a plan. To make a plan you can use a spreadsheet, a calendar, or just a piece of paper. Always start any long term plan with your end goal and work your way backwards to the present day. I go month by month for my long-term plans and then extrapolate my weekly plans and todo's from the long-term plan to keep me on track as I go. It really works. I have done this for every major project or campaign that I have led, and this is how we planned our quest to rent-to-own our home. We planned for 18 months, and it ended up taking us 27 months, but that is how plans work: they will almost always change. Had we made our plan before we found our home it would have been a three or four year plan. As long as the goals are realistic and they remain the path, the plan to get there should be flexible enough to change. If you are able to pivot and adapt then you know you are still on the right pathway to achieving your goal. Planning tools are also available on the Rent2OwnBook.com website so you can get some ideas for plans and planning templates.

It is also a good idea to print out any credit card bills that you have and keep them in your file. If you use them responsibly, credit cards can help you build the type of credit that gives the bank confidence in loaning a lot of money to you. They can also easily block you from getting a line of credit to buy your home. Because of this they are to be thought of as a tool to build your credit score, not as a way to buy things for which you might be short on cash. Keep a balance on them that you can easily pay off at a moment's notice. Too much debt will affect your debt-to-income ratio which is the main piece of the puzzle for a bank deciding whether or not to give you a home loan. If you carry too much credit card debt to pay off easily then for every swipe of plastic, your savings shrinks and you look riskier and riskier to a lender. That balance that sits on your credit card, especially if you have a higher interest rate, is costing you valuable interest payments to the bank that holds your card. As they charge interest on the balance it is like a siphon sucking directly out of your savings account.

For each credit card bill, write a draft plan for how you will simultaneously pay off your credit cards and start a little savings. It is not easy. For some it will not be possible. You may need a year or two of getting rid of credit cards and paying down credit card debt before you even start looking at potential homes. That is the reality of credit cards. If you use them responsibly, they can help you build your credit up to become a more attractive candidate for a home loan, or you can treat them like actual money and they will sink your future. Avoid running them up at all costs. Do not buy things that you want with them. I never carried them, but Allison did. She had to pay off a reasonable balance of $2,500 in order to set up a debt-to-income ratio that would put us in the best possible position to get approved for a home loan. $2500 was an easy amount for us to pay off. It did not set us back to a point in which it hurt our savings. From that point forward, if she paid for something with her credit card she paid it off as soon as the bill came without ever carrying a balance of more than $300.

This is a lot of work. Ignoring your debt and waiting to start your savings until you need it can derail your efforts to close on your loan, or it will allow someone who has saved enough for an option payment to sneak ahead of you and get into the home you want. In the beginning you have more time to work on these things. You are able to use the positive energy and excitement that is flowing through you to get this ball rolling. By starting to be a person who takes action, you will start the good habit of being the person who gets it done rather than the person who puts it off until another day. You will thank yourself dozens of times for starting this now and then sticking to it.

Here is what you need to do: Get a folder of some kind and a safe place to keep this sensitive information. Start by putting your last W-2 and paystubs in there. Request a credit report, and put that in the folder too. Look at any negative marks on the credit report and begin writing letters to yourself explaining how they happened. Once you have very rough drafts of those letters, make a plan, including goals, for how you are going to get each of those marks paid and/or removed in the next 18 to 20 months. Keep all of this in your file, and add the rest of the documents as you go. I made our plan by starting at the end point, October of 2013, and working backwards to build a timeline for what we would need to do to close in October. Do not be afraid to amend your plan as you go, but stick with your goals and do not compromise the end goal. These first steps are the first you should be taking as you begin your rent-to-own journey.

Chapter Checklist:
1. Start taking action right now by finding or buying some kind of folder or filing system (use paper for your file, electronic for backup).

2. Include the following:
____Any credit card bills.

___Draft plans to pay off credit cards.

___Last W-2.

___Most recent pay stubs.

___Most recent credit report.

___First drafts of letters explaining any negatives on your credit.

___A draft plan for how to address and fix each one of those negative marks.

___Documentation for any additional assets.

3. Write your first draft plan for your home starting with your end goal.

___Do not feel pressure to fill it all in. You can do that as you read the book.

___Just get your goal down on paper and start getting the documents together.

___Make a plan for each and every task associated with getting your home. They will come together to become your master plan.

___Find a safe place for your file and back it up electronically even if you have to find a friend with a scanner or go to a print shop.

"Do not save what is left after spending, but spend what is left after saving."

Warren Buffet

SAVING MONEY

Saving money is hard. Lots of people would much rather you spent all of the money you earn because there is a chance they will get some of it. Understand that very few people care if you save a penny. Even fewer want you to. You are the only real lock and key on your piggy bank. That is correct; you have to be the lock on your piggy bank. There is just no other way to save. As of now there is no app or service that will make you save money. Please remember that because without serious discipline in saving money you will not be able to complete a rentto-own purchase. Every time you decide to "tap into your savings" you are cutting right to the front of the line of people who want your money. Why do that? There are millions of reasons, and you can convince yourself that any one of those reasons justifies depleting your savings. Just remember to ask yourself two important questions before finishing that withdrawal: 1.) is this money going to move me further towards getting my home than if it was sitting in the bank to become my down payment?2.) Is someone in my family dependent on this money to survive? If you answered yes to both of these, then do what you have to do. In reality you will find very few answers justify a yes to Question One as without a down payment you do not get a house. Question Two makes certain that family always comes first. If you throw them away and get your house, it will be a lonely and unhappy place to live.

Right now is the best time to start a savings account. This is priority number one because rent-toown agreements almost always require an option payment to the seller up front. That is in addition to the down payment you will need to make to the bank in order to get a home loan. Two down payments could sound a little scary. Before you say forget this rent-to-own stuff and its double down payment, consider that the first payment is to the seller and is part of the agreement to buy the home, and the second likely comes years later and goes to the bank at closing. It is not as impossible or scary as it might sound. In many agreements, in order to protect the seller if you do not close the deal on your lease option home they keep your initial down payment money. This is not cheap as the option money is typically 3% of the current value of the home. In our case it was $7000 as our home when we signed the initial contract was worth $240,000. If you do not start saving right now, you will likely not have enough to make the option payment in order to even get started. This could be painful as rent-to-own homes are not always easy to find and waiting to save up a down payment or scrambling at the last minute could provide an opportunity for someone who has been disciplined in building savings to jump ahead of you and get the home you want.

We started our savings early because we thought that we could be considered for a traditional mortgage. Was it embarrassing and difficult to have mortgage brokers ignore us or hold back laughter as they asked us to leave? Yes it was, but it worked well for us because we had almost all of the $7000 that our rent-to-own seller (the homeowner) required to get us into the home, so we were able to jump on the deal right away when we found it. Had we waited to start saving until we found a rent-to-own home it would have taken weeks to save up the $7,000 and we would have certainly lost our opportunity; the homeowner had a number of other interested renters responding to his ad.

Saving money early on in the process also got us on a committed budget. Do not downplay this. We did not live lavishly, but we also did not have a good saving culture built into our relationship. Habits are hard to break and even harder to start, so learning how to save up more money than you thought you could early is a key component to saving up enough over the long haul. Start now and keep saving. If you do, you will get good at it, and you cannot buy your house unless you get good at saving money.

If you are reading this because you have a low credit score, you will need to save a lot more money to buy your home. Even if you improve your credit, the negative history will likely be used against you and banks will want you to cough up a little more to give them the peace of mind that you can repay what you borrow. You will also have to rehab your credit. We believe rehabilitating your credit and saving your saving money work best when you do them together, and we will share how that worked for us in the credit chapter. A general rule to keep in mind is the lower your credit score, the more money you will need to save toward your down payment. Lease option agreements, which is the wonky way to say rent-to-own contracts, often have a date at which the agreement terminates. This makes it more difficult to save enough money as it takes time to build a savings.

The first thing you have to do is to stop reading here and open a savings account and deposit at least $100. If you have already done this or have a savings account you are going to use, please stop reading and put at least another $100 in there right now. If you have online banking this should only take a few minutes.

From here we will assume that you now have a budding savings.

I hope that is a good feeling. If it is not a good feeling it could be that you are feeling stress, and if there is stress now in your budget then saving money may not be a good feeling. This is something that you need to begin to fix right now. Figure out why saving money is causing you stress and whatever reason you find, deal with that right now. In order to create a new habit of saving money it has to feel really good to watch your account grow. When you get to that place you will know you are on your way to getting a down payment for your home.

If you are feeling stress about saving money, go back to the opening chapter and make sure that you are not the cause of your stress. No matter what the cause, you have got to figure out how to stop it. In fact, not only do you have to stop that stressful feeling, but you have to totally reverse it. Saving money should feel great! If you are the cause of your own stress (and I know I was in my case) you can easily go to the source and fix it. Remember that you are at once both the hero of your rent-to-own story and your biggest enemy to reaching your goal of closing on your rent-to-own home.

Is the stress all in your mind? You might be creating a story in your mind that you may not have enough money for gas if you save, and if you can't get to work you will lose your job, and you can't save money without a job! This is all wrong. Stop thinking that way. That stress is likely caused by doubt creating a vision of a tragedy. Visions of personal tragedy and ruin cause the wrong kind of chemical reactions in your brain (see Olivia Fox's book, The Charisma Myth). You can easily convince yourself that those made up situations are really actually going to happen to you, or are happening to you. If that is how you approach your rent-to-own situation you are taking a far more difficult path.

There are lots of reasons that you might feel stress around saving money, but you have to identify them, deal with them and flip that fear, doubt and stress around. Remember that your desire and drive to own a home has to overcome your fears. You have to want it more than that made up story in your head, and if you do want it badly you can create a new reality. Create a story in which you ask someone to loan you $10 to $20 for gas to get you through. You still have that $100 in your savings account, and then after you get paid and pay your friend back, you double your savings by adding another $100! Rather than believing the personal tragedy story you create, you will start to believe this new crazy story in your head that you can become a homeowner. After all, you got the idea, you found this book, and you are already saving for your home. Create a reality in which you save a little bit every paycheck, and remember that every great quest starts with one small step. If you can't put all $100 in this month, shoot for $20 or even just $10. Your savings will still be growing. Eventually when you get through those tough times and you still have your slow growing little savings account, you will realize that you really can do it, and it will start to be a good feeling to have a growing savings.

Another important tool to saving is making a budget. A lot of people will tell you that budgets are over-rated. They'll point out that nobody likes them and nobody actually sticks to them anyway. That may be true in a lot of cases, but we had to buckle down and create budgets that worked for us. Remember to take calculated risks. A budget is an important part of making that calculation.

In order to create a budget I had to start by setting a realistic savings goal. To do that I used a mortgage calculator to see an estimate of what kind of a down payment I would need for the prices of homes in Seattle. You can find these calculators all over the internet but I include a free one for you at Rent2OwnBook.com. In general you will need a 20% down payment on your mortgage to close on your home. In our case that was $40,000. A rent-to-own agreement is typically 24 months, and so we knew we needed to get to that goal a little before the full 24 months. We also understood that other things could come up along the way that could set us back on our savings goals. That led me to come up with a savings guide that worked for us.

You should be able to save 20% in 24 months, so a goal of 1% per month is a good guide to follow. If you make it without incident then you get the bonus of saving an extra 4%. It is more realistic that things will come up like a $3000 vet bill (this happened to us). Because "life" happens, planning for that extra 4% cushion will help you absorb any potential setbacks along the way. If you cannot budget for 1% per month on your current salary or wage then you are aiming too high, and you can't afford that house. Realistic goals feel great because you can make a realistic plan and then see it coming to fruition day after day. Unrealistic goals will make things feel impossible. Considering how hard it is to get your home, you will want to be as realistic as you can. Do not make it any harder than it has to be. If your credit is good you will likely need a significantly lower down payment. If your credit is ok-to-good and your home passes an FHA inspection, you can get financed through the Federal Housing Authority which will also require a much lower down payment.

There are some great free tools out there for setting up a budget. Washington state requires that first-time home buyers attend a class designed to help potential buyers avoid common pitfalls and find success. We actually found this to be a pretty good class, and recommend you find a free one to attend even if it is not required where you live. One take away from the class we felt made it worth the time is the free budget tool they give away. It was as good as anything we found in our search and really makes managing your income and saving money much easier. Before keeping a tight budget it was like fumbling around in the dark, impossible to save any money. A budget makes it all possible. It is a necessary cog in the savings machine. It really surprised us how much money was frivolously spent that could have been added to our growing savings account.

If you do not have access to a free class for first time homebuyers or feel you really do not need that, try searching online. There are smartphone apps that have budget tools, websites, and services. Try as many as it takes until you find the budget tool that helps you see a path to saving and motivates you to stick to it.

What I found that worked best was to use budget tools to identify where we were spending money that we should have been saving and then change that behavior. From there the budgets that actually worked and were easy to stick to were quarterly budgets. Trying to create a one-size-fits-all budget would not work for me. At different times of the year my capacity to save changes. From January to May I can save the most. Heating costs go up in the winter which can cut into savings a bit, but overall my expenses are less during the late winter and early spring. My budget during the first two quarters of the year would be broken down with more money being put into savings than the last quarter of the year when there are holidays that can become very expensive. As long as I could put any money away during that last quarter of the year I was happy. In a lot of cases simply surviving the last quarter of the year without depleting my savings was as much of a victory as adding anything at all.

How I approached this quarterly budget was not to micro-manage myself either. I tried to only focus on the big picture rather than beat myself up over buying a latte. I knew that I would make about $15,000 per quarter. I knew my bills and expenses were about $7,000 per quarter. So I knew I could set my budget to save at least $6,500 per quarter in the first two months of the year. In the summer quarter I usually had family come to visit and would take vacation and ultimately spend a bit more freely, so I would shoot to save at least $2,000. The winter quarter for us is expensive. There are 3 major holidays, a birthday, a lot of travel, gift giving and phone calls. Saving was more limited during this time, but the first two quarters usually more than made up for the holiday splurges. If we could save $500 to $1000 in the winter quarter we both felt like that was a big victory, and so did our savings account.

These quarterly goals are essential to making a budget, and they should tie right into your overall savings goal based on that 1% per month savings guide. Setting that realistic goal is one of the most important tools to getting your home. It is worth every bit of your time to formulate and set that realistic goal. When you set calculated goals that have a measurable result and actionable plans, your goals make you work hard to stay on track because you can see your saving grow just as planned. That is one key to closing the deal. It's worth noting that if you set an impossible goal you may confuse your goal setting error with the self-destructive belief that it is impossible to buy your home. That could be a costly mistake.

Another part of setting up your budget and goal is to examine exactly how much you have been paid over the past 2 years. Get your last two w-2's together and take the average you have made over the last two years. You will need these down the road anyway, so if you have not yet done this put these in your documents file. The average you get from these is the number you should use to formulate your budget. Do not plan on a raise you have not gotten yet. Plan for what you have made and treat any bonus or raise as extra savings.

Allison and I used an average of $45,000 as that was Allison's average salary over the two years leading up to when we made our plan. We stuck to that baseline even when our combined incomes were $105,000 per year. We did this because we already built a plan around Allison's income as our calculations said she could afford this home based on those parameters. It worked out to where she could not close at that salary and we had to combine our incomes. Because my credit was still poor we were pressured by our first lending institution to increase our down payment regularly.

That was stressful and caused us to fail over and over as we attempted to close for months. Eventually my credit rebounded enough and we did it, but even good credit would not have gotten us into our home without our disciplined budget and savings.

Now you have already started saving for your option payment and perhaps even your down payment/ escrow payment and you know what you can afford, you know how much you have to save, and you have a budget to get there, and in doing so you are keeping all important documents in the file you created. If you have good credit, or a plan to improve your credit, then you are ready to start searching for a home.

As you work through this process, understand that there will be many other interests that compete with your savings. Things will pop up all of the time that will try to convince you to tap into the savings just this once for a little bit of money. Do your best to stay focused on locking that savings up to where money only flows into it. It will become contagious at some point, and the momentum you gain as your hard earned savings piles up will keep you moving toward attaining your home.

Chapter Checklist:

___Start a savings account right away. If you can, do it before moving on to Chapter 2.

___Put at least $100 in your new savings.

___If you already have a savings account building, add an extra $100 to it (the point is to challenge yourself to become good at saving money).

___Set a savings goal based on being able to save 1% of the purchase price per month with a goal to get to 24%.

___Create a budget for the next year.

___Create a general budget for each quarter by subtracting your expenses from your net pay and by saving as much of the left over income as you possibly can.

___Identify the quarters in which you can save the most and really buckle down in those, giving yourself the freedom to let things like holidays have their share of your income.

___Stick to your budget. Meeting those goals means that over the course of the year you will become better with your hard-earned money and it will feel good to save it and possibly even become contagious.

> "Every financial worry you want to banish and financial dream you want to achieve comes from taking tiny steps today that put you on a path toward your goals."
>
> Suze Orman

CREDIT

If you are reading this and your credit score is halfway decent, meaning over 640, then you might have some work to do to make your credit good or great and then to keep it that way, but you are well on your way to being able to close the deal on a rentto-own home. Credit is the key that unlocks the front door to your home. There are a lot of factors that you need but without a good credit score you will have to buy everything paid in full and in cold, hard cash. That was not an option for us or for most people.

Our credit was pretty bad, but we made a great team to fix it. What Allison and I did was use our rent-to-own purchase as a way to rehabilitate our credit. We did this primarily because we had to rehabilitate our credit in order to close the deal because we needed bank financing through a home loan to meet the $212,700 price tag. That is a lot of money to ask for, so making a plan to rehabilitate our credit in realistic time with our end goal to get bank financing was essential. What happened was that getting to build a life while living in our goal (our home) helped keep us ultra-focused on continuing to do the hard work necessary to rehabilitate our credit. I never found a better motivation than coming home to my dream home, in my dream neighborhood, in my dream city, everyday. I got in the habit of asking myself upon seeing it, "Did I take care of everything I had to today to move my credit forward?" The answer was not always yes but just staying accountable to myself made more yes's than no's. I had already started the credit rehabilitation process, but finding our rent-to-own home was the game changer that kicked my motivation into high gear.

Do not give up on your credit before you get started because if you are like Allison and I were then you have debt and you have bad, even hopeless credit. With debt you will have to pay it down to a level that does not limit your home buying power. You can pay on your debts and get them in order while saving money and rehabilitating your credit. These are not mutually exclusive. Given this rent-toown experience I have found that saving money and paying down debt went together for us in a way that made each happen fast enough for us to own a home.

How hopeless was hopeless?

In 2007, after three years of poverty wages as a teaching assistant at a major research university, my wife had filed for bankruptcy. She had $17,000 in credit card debt because she mistakenly thought that she could supplement a $13,000 a year stipend with credit cards, and then pay them swiftly off each quarter with student loans. It was a financial shell game and she was a big loser: As her credit card debt rose, her ability to access student loans dropped dramatically, and soon she was sending all of her tiny stipend to her credit cards just to stay afloat while using her credit cards to pay her bills, incurring more debt and fees every month until she felt crushed under the weight of them. And she was a proud, educated and supposedly responsible person. It went against everything she stood for to file for bankruptcy. It felt like stealing to have that debt wiped away. Thankfully, she recognized that to be a homeowner some day, she was going to have to make hard choices, some of them counter-intuitive, to rebuild her credit, her financial health, and her self-esteem.

Bankruptcy was designed and is intended to be a court of last resort to protect consumers and keep our economy solvent. Many successful millionaires and billionaires even use it as a shrewd business practice to keep themselves moving forward. Donald Trump, for example, has filed for bankruptcy four times. What bankruptcy is not is a "get out of jail free card" or an experience anyone (other than a multimillionaire) would want to go through more than once. Because she filed for bankruptcy in 2007, she couldn't rent an apartment without a co-signer until 2009. She was barely able to buy a car in 2010, and then at ridiculous interest rates. She wasn't eligible to be considered for a home loan until 2014, a full seven years later. I'm not sharing her story because I want to scare you, or to advocate bankruptcy as a viable option for you in your rent-to-own journey; it's not). I just want you to know that no matter how hopeless your situation may seem, odds are it was not as hopeless as ours.

How Hopeless was Hopeless? Part 2

In my situation, I had let my student loans go. It took a long time to land a decent job. It took months to get any job at all after college. When I did, it paid $9/hr for hard work in a toothpaste factory. Packaging toothpaste meant looking directly down at toothpaste and their boxes for hours. My neck would cramp to the point of headaches that could only be remedied by laying my head down to rest. At lunch I would go to my car to lay my head down and the supervisor would come out to tell me that I was not allowed to sleep in the car because it looked bad, even though this place was out in rural Florida so there was nobody around to even see me but him. I tried to explain to him that I was not sleeping, but he didn't believe that I was just resting my neck to aid a headache. I was driving a borrowed, gas guzzling car to that nine dollar per hour job and the only thing that made that car worth anything was that it had the space for me to lie down to relax my neck.

My coworkers used to pack extra lunches for me and invite me over to their homes for dinner. They treated me so well because after I was forced to sit in the break room they saw that I would often have little to eat at lunch anyway. Something about sharing food builds relationships and creates an environment that one day got us all talking about our pay. We all found out that I was paid one dollar per hour more than the women and people of color who were working with me; I was the only white male not in management. I was never more ashamed at a job. They were feeding me because I was struggling to afford food, but I was making more money than them. The pain in that job hurt me in many ways, and one of the most significant was that I couldn't afford to pay my student loans.

I finally did get a good job nearly one full year after graduation. It might be one of the best jobs I have ever had. Alachua County CHOICES was a county-funded health insurance program for the working uninsured living in Alachua County, FL. It has since been replaced by the Affordable Care Act (ACA) and is no longer in existence, but if you had a job and lived in Alachua County and met a certain percentage of the poverty standard you could visit one of our organizers and we would set you up into the program. At the time the program had dozens of doctors and about one dozen dentists all ready to see new patients. I loved helping people get health insurance. It was challenging but rewarding, especially because I went eight years without any health insurance myself until I landed the job at CHOICES.

On multiple occasions at events around Alachua County I had people approach me who I helped get into the program, and I did not even work there very long. They would give me big hugs and tell me how much I helped them and their families. One woman was crying while telling me she had hoped to run into me someday. She said she was so desperate when we first met that she had completely given up and expected to die. Because I filled out the paperwork for her and helped her enroll, she was able to manage her chronic illness and live a quality of life that at last allowed her to keep a job more than a few months. That meant she could leave homelessness behind for good. I had no idea taking a few minutes to fill out a form for someone who needed health insurance could make such an impact on someone's world. After the toothpaste job I was in heaven working at CHOICES. Since I have found out that the Alachua County CHOICES program has been replaced by the ACA (ObamaCare) I have learned another disturbing piece of news: For some reason Florida lawmakers rejected Federal funds for Medicaid expansion that was available through the ACA, leaving thousands who were in the CHOICES program again without access to health insurance. I believe I could have done amazing work at CHOICES and probably have lived a good life, but a failing marriage and divorce forced me out of that job after just a few months. It was devastating.

My credit was taking knock out blows. I had no idea how to defend myself and I hit the mat hard, just in time for the economy to crash like a roundhouse to the temple, hitting me while I was already down. With no one in my corner I was simply down for the count with no vision or strategy for how to get back up. I tired several times to get a handle on it all, including my student loans. It was hard to make an impact on anything when I was flat broke and flat on my back far away from home with no support system.

It did not take long to get used to the harassing phone calls either. I would answer when I could, but usually my phone looked as if it was ringing all day long while I was at work as I would sometimes have more than one dozen collection calls in an eight hour period. I would call around to figure out why, but usually the number that I would call back was an automated response telling me to call back during business hours. When I did get to talk to someone they usually only knew about one or two loans that their bank held and were limited to what they could do for me.

Getting Up and Fighting Back

As I mentioned, if getting my credit pummeled with my own bad decisions, no good jobs, and a divorce was not bad enough, the economy crashed less than one year later. I should have been knocked out, but I simply refused to give up because I believed so deeply in what I could accomplish. There was no way I was going to let a made-up thing like a silly three-digit credit number hold me back. Recognizing that I needed to make a change, I started to learn how to do it right. This was not easy. Remember, I was often my own worst enemy in all of this and facing and correcting my own bad habits was hard. I recognized it was time to do the hard work. I had to start it first. That is not to say that I did not get help. I did and I needed it.

I had seventeen loans and I was late on almost all of the them. Eleven were in default which is why no credit agency would consolidate for me. Juggling seventeen loans was still causing me to miss payments, and on top of that they were often being bought and sold by other banks, making it even more difficult to stay on top of who to pay and where my payments were going.

It was so overwhelming that even when I would make the commitment to buckle down and pay them, I would get stuck just trying to figure out where to start. It seemed like nobody wanted to help someone in my situation. I learned that I had to start calling at 5 am because if I got in too late east coast time I had wait times over 30 minutes and offices that often were closed or would disconnect me, forcing me to start all over again. As a young professional trying to make it in a demanding job I did not have a lot of time to sit around all day trying to act like my own accountant. I often had to say, "it is either me sitting around all day trying to pay one loan or going to work to earn enough money to pay on all of them." This was a bad attitude, but I am sharing it with you to help you to avoid the same poisonous thoughts. I was made to feel like less of a person because of this little number, and it felt like all other factors were working against my ability to fix it.

The loans that I could pay online were extremely difficult to pay. The layers of log-in security were cryptic and often seemed impossible, and even when I would write down my usernames, passwords and security questions for each site, it seemed like they would change them from month to month without telling me. This happened every month, and if I tried to log in and failed three times in a row with my correct password they would lock me out of the entire website like a criminal. I would have to start a whole new account for myself which takes much longer than simply logging in and paying because it requires setting up my bank routing information again as well as all of the other information that goes with creating an online identity. This is just another reason why it is helpful to create folders with all of this information when you are getting started. At one point Allison did not believe that this was happening to me month after month, so she created a file with all of my passwords and usernames for each site. When she tried to log-in for me the passwords that she set up and filed away failed to let us in. It was frustrating but at least someone else got to experience how broken and difficult the online payment system was.

In some cases getting locked out would also put me on long tech support calls in which they would have to set up an entirely new account for me. I would have to reset my information all the time. When you are on the west coast and banks back east buy your loans, they expect you to get up for their business hours: 4am until noon, or sometimes 2pm. It is a small window to deal with big credit problems. When I asked someone on a tech support call if other people have pointed out to them that it makes no sense to lock us out of paying our debt, as nobody is trying to steal my debt the helpful person laughed and said, "everyone says that."

During this weekly process of getting almost nowhere on my loans, I found out that some loans were in default. By some I mean a majority, eleven of them. Others were in late status, and some others were constantly bought by other banks, and in one case the old bank went out of business leaving an unpaid notice on my credit report even though the loan was paid in full before another bank purchased it. It must not occur to a bank that they are potentially ruining someone's life when they leave notices like that on people's credit rating and they go out of business. It is yet another example of how oppressive it is to be poor.

I tried consolidation in the first few years after graduation and no company would accept me. I was already late on some loans and did not even know it. Juggling seventeen payments was like a part-time accountant job, but trying to deal with eleven of them in default would take hours out of some of my workdays. This meant a lot of working late into the night when others were comfortably home in bed. My investment in my education seemed like a very bad decision for years.

This was all very painful and took a lot of time. I had many offers from people to help me. It ended up that I only took help from two people, a friend and my wife, as it became clear to me at some point that others were embarrassed for me when they saw my credit report, so I made sure to hide it and stopped seeking out help. It may seem horrifying to you to read this, and it should. I cannot stress how painful this all was. I am so happy as I sit here now for having gone through it. I shutter to think of where my life would be right now had I not been willing to get some credit help and pull myself together to do the hard and painful work of cleaning up my credit.

First, to get things going I had to rehabilitate my student loans. For a time there was no way for people in my hopeless position to rehabilitate their defaulted loans until student loan reforms were passed. These reforms created pathways for those of us hardest hit by the student loan crisis to start over by creating programs that helped to organize many loans into one payment and allow me to pay them all down for a defined period of time. After that time the company running the programs would delete the defaults from my credit record.

This is a great program for people like me who now are able and intend to pay loans but are blocked by their one time inability to do so. Rehabilitating loans did get eleven of them into one consolidated and affordable payment. That was a huge help. Then removing the negatives from my credit report was an even bigger help.

Beyond allowing those of us with lots of defaults to rehabilitate, I was extremely fortunate that President

Obama passed a six-month temporary window to allow students and graduates in my situation to consolidate our student loan debt. There are many different consolidation services. My situation was particularly hopeless and most consolidation services refused to help me. Hopefully you will not need a law to help you get out of debt. My wife was also a big help with this process, and together we got my very unmanageable seventeen loans and very high monthly total payment into two very manageable payments of consolidated loans. I went from up to $1100 monthly to $225.

Many of these programs were temporary. Depending on when you read this the climate around student loan reforms could be much different. Hopefully any changes are for the better as the current student loan system is totally broken. Do not sit by passively if you have student loan problems; take action. Find out what is there to help you, weigh all of your options, and get going on the best ones. Waiting will only make it worse. Taking action, even and especially on those first few crucial steps, and following through is the hardest part.

You will have to deal with your debt and your credit if you are going to buy a home via a rent-toown agreement. There are many different companies and non-profits that are out there to help you. Just like anything, many of them will charge a fee. This can get tricky because you are also working hard to be disciplined with your savings, so paying someone to help you rehab your credit has to be affordable enough to not cut into your savings plan. Do not just pick the least expensive debt company or the first you find. Do research and ask around for any first hand experience with companies who assist with debt. Our credit union helped us with this for free. They set up an appointment on a Saturday and reviewed our credit report line by line for three hours giving us helpful suggestions for how we can improve our credit and debt load.

Part of debt management is adjusting payments and consolidating others or paying off some altogether. It is also important to note that when you are in this part of your search and you are setting up monthly payments to set them up at the lowest level possible. Lenders will want to review your debt-toincome ratio. Very simply put, this is how much you make per month compared to how much you owe per month. If the ratio is poor, meaning much of your income going to bills, it will be harder to save enough money anyway so your incentive will always be to pay the lowest amount possible while keeping the lowest possible debt. It might feel better to set a higher payment, but when a lender assesses your ability to pay that good feeling will prevent you from closing on your home.

Here is a list of what I had to do:
- Refinance my car. My payment went from $369/month to$150/month.
- Pay down any credit cards: If the balance was $1500 or less our rule was to pay it off. If you have several cards,

concentrate on paying off the one with the highest interest rate first, then the next-highest interest rate card, and so on. You can pay $5 more than the minimum balance on the others, and as long as you're not using your cards and creating new debt, your balances will decrease.

- Consolidate student loans At the time I did this I could have set my monthly payment lower, and would have if I had to do it over again.
- Save as much money as possible! The more you can afford to put down, the less your mortgage payment will be, making your debt-to-income ratio much more appealing to a lender.
- Get health insurance Medical bills can really block you from attaining your home. If you find yourself in need of help, ask for charity. Go to hospitals that offer charity care and do not be afraid to ask for this.
- Negotiate your hospital bills down to what you can afford. If you do owe hospital bills, you already know that hospitals are much more concerned with collecting payment than they are with your personal health. Reduce your bills any way possible.

Here's what I didn't do, but Allison did:

I mentioned earlier that my wife filed for bankruptcy in 2007. It's counter-intuitive, but a part of her climb back into credit worthiness was to go right back to the snake that bit her, a new credit account. It is true that carrying a small amount of debt (and never more than 1/3 of the credit limit, so if you have a card with a $1000 limit, never carry a balance of more than $300) will rapidly improve your credit score if you pay more than the minimum payment each month and never miss a payment. Banks want you to do this; that's how they make their money. I just couldn't bring myself to do it. Having and using credit cards, responsibly or not, is just not a good idea for me. Even when our banker, when negotiating our loan with his underwriter, suggested I use this strategy to hurry my credit rehabilitation process along, I stuck to my guns, and I'm glad to say I reached my goal without compromising my principles.

Having and using a small amount of credit responsibly may do wonders for your credit score (well, at least according to my wife's experience), but what will NOT work and defeat your savings goal and possibly even cause you greater credit score headaches in the future is to enter into one of those magic bullet credit rehabilitation programs. If a person or program makes the claim that they can raise your credit score in a short amount of time, run, don't walk, to your bank and put that money towards paying off your balance instead. Be very careful with these companies. They prey upon people desperate to make the collection harassment stop. There are reputable services, but you have to search and research to find them. In our case, the one-time (free) consultation with our credit union was enough to get the information we needed to rehabilitate our credit scores ourselves.

A lot of very good financial advisers will tell you to pay your debts before working to save money. This is excellent advice in many instances, but not a blanket solution that fits everyone. If you are saving for a house there are other factors that come into play. If you are in a stable and affordable living situation then there is not a lot of urgency to save money so you can sit tight and pay down your debts and rehab your credit. If you are in a housing market in which prices are not going up and there is an abundance of homes on the market, you have time to work on your debts as well. In our case, Seattle's market was and is booming. If we had waited until we paid down our debts, we would have been completely priced out of buying any home in Seattle. That advice just did not work for us. You will surprise yourself. As good as it feels to build a savings to buy a home, it feels even better when you manage your debts and build your savings. Saving money really did become much, much easier once the hard work of debt management was behind us. But in hindsight it was not until we had the opportunity of a lifetime to get into our rent-to-own home, coupled with risk management, that we had something that forced us to immediately start saving money for that option payment and eventual down payment. We needed that money fast so we had to look at where that savings was going to come from, and it had to come from getting a handle on our debt.

Having the goal of home ownership as our focus and a need to immediately start a savings really made managing our seemingly hopeless debt and credit far easier. We had to save money and it had to come from somewhere, so we focused on managing our debts, and from that debt management our savings emerged. It all works together if you have goals and plans to achieve them.

So now you know how bad our situation was and our strategy to get out. It was some of the hardest work I have ever done, but it worked and it worked well and relatively quickly. Nobody can prescribe one solution to your credit. It is yours and you are going to know your own situation far better than anyone else so you are your best expert. You are your best adviser and motivator.

Here is what I recommend that you do:

Start by getting a folder together just for your credit. Keep it with your documents folder. You are going to have to account for every credit negative whether you fixed it or not, so start writing explanations for each one. We eventually learned this through trial and error.

Next, start answering those collection calls if you are getting them. Find out who is calling about what and what it is that you owe. Tell them you need information because you are starting a debt management program. Add this information to your folder. If you can pay them something now try to offer them what you can afford to pay.

Now you will need to get your free yearly credit report. Get the detailed full report. Make a copy and put it in your file. Then go item by item and figure out the what, where and why about each collection and outline those aspects for each bad mark. This is important because it will make the next steps much easier. It helped us a lot to sit down with a representative from our credit union who did this with us step by step.

Then the tedious part: write a letter for each mark. Use your outline from doing your research or meeting with your bank or credit union on each collection or negative mark. You will need these letters when you close anyway as the bank will keep a record of your explanation for each negative. Had we known right from the beginning, we could have written these early and pulled them from our file as we went. This would have avoided the headache of having to go back and recall old credit negatives and write letters which held us up on our first closing attempt.

Now is the time when you are knee deep in the often painful credit rehab process, so now is really the best time to write these letters anyway. In the letter you will have to explain as much as you know about the negative mark on your credit, why it happened, and why it will never happen again. This is actually good practice for you anyway. It really gets you thinking about your debts and helps you get a vision for better management from this point forward. If you are looking at it correctly, it should also get you feeling some accountability for your part of the responsibility of each negative mark on your credit. Experiencing that sense of accountability should be a good feeling. It allows you to finally take ownership of the debt and the plan you make to get it managed. This is important because no one will do this for you. At least not without you paying them a lot of money, and even then they will make you actually do most of the hard work of rehabilitating your credit.

When you make your plan, start with how long you want it to take to get your credit rehabilitated. In reality it took me almost three years to raise my score 40 to 100 points depending on the credit reporting agency. Use my story and how long it took as a gauge for your own situation. If you truly believe you can do it in two years, then make a two year plan. Start at the end goal and work your way backwards through your plan. This book is about one goal, home ownership, so starting with that end goal and working back makes sure that your plan is focused solely on your goal of home ownership.

I cannot give you a lot of specifics about your own personal plans. It takes a deep understanding of your situation. There is one part of the plan that you will need to include on every month, week, and day, and that is paying your bills on time. When it comes time to close on your house one missed payment can do you in, and it will take a year of on-time payments to make up for one missed payment. This may not seem fair, but it is how the banks will judge your credit worthiness, so that is one part of your credit rehabilitation plan I can tell you to include everywhere.

Credit was the most painful part of this for me. It is important to note that I started rehabilitating my credit, long before we even started our search for rent-to-own homes. If your credit is bad there is no better day than today to start going in the other direction. Waiting another day will not help you get your home. I started down that hard road in 2009. Had I waited until we found our home in 2012 there would not have been enough time for me to get my credit in order to close the deal on our rent-to-own home. Please make certain that your plan to rehabilitate your credit is realistic with the timeline necessary to close on your home. You want to set yourself up to take your best shot, not for failure. Remember it is about taking calculated risks. A good calculated risk requires taking time to strategize everything you do.

Another reason credit was so painful for me is because I don't buy things that I can't afford. I never have. My parents didn't do this, and following their example was easy for me. I didn't have any other examples of people using credit to live beyond their means in my life either. My examples were all people who lived below their means, and worked extremely hard to do it. I always thought that a credit score was intended to identify those people who couldn't use credit responsibly. In my case if that is still what credit is used for, then perhaps I truly was priced out of an education as the only times in my life when I accessed credit were to fund my pursuit of higher education in some way.

Even though I do not have a history of buying things that I can't afford and that behavior didn't help my credit score, it was a big help to me during our rent-to-own journey. It made living below my means easy for me. For example it was easy for me to live without cable. I got us a digital antenna for $20 and we got 36 HD channels! Add the internet to that antenna and low cost quality entertainment is easy to come by. I never felt left out of any water cooler conversations about the new hit show, movie or sporting event.

You don't have to be a complete shut-in to live below your means. You can live a happy life. Stick to your budget and your goals. Live within your means as you rent-to-own. This "only buy it if you can afford to save money first" attitude was another key element to getting our home. I always prioritized home ownership over my car or clothes or computer or gadgets.

Buying your home will be no different. Be realistic about what you can afford. Do not give up on yourself as you take on the hard work of rehabilitating your credit. Do not take your rent-toown home for granted. Find a way to remind yourself each day that you value home ownership over all else except family. That is reason enough to soldier through another painful day of having to do the extremely hard work of fixing your credit. You can do it. If you know you need to improve your credit start right now. Once you get your credit rehabilitated you will thank yourself over and over again for taking that all important first step and sticking with it. While you are re-habbing your credit adopt a lifestyle of living below your means and saving money as it will help your credit and it will help you get your home.

How to Report Your Rent-to-Own Payments on Your Credit Report

A recent discovery for me that I wish we would have had when we started renting our home is RentBu-reau. RentBureau is a credit reporting company now owned by Experian which means that you can now get your rental payments toward your home reported on your Experian credit report. Experian is one of the major credit reporting companies and any addition help to rebuilding credit is valuable especially if you are trying to rebuild your credit in time to meet a termination date. It certainly would have helped us and I will take you through how you can use it to help your on-time rent-to-own payments help you rebuild your credit score.

There are four companies that report to RentBureau:
https://www.clearnow.com
http://www.williampaid.com
http://www.renttrack.com
http://www.payyourrent.com

You will have to ask the seller or landlord to report to this. Let them know that it will help you and that helps them too in that it gives you added incentive to get your rent payments in on time each month. It is worth the extra time to set up the automatic payments through one of these websites so that they always know exactly when they are getting paid and know that it will be there every time.

Each of these companies are a little different with the services that they offer. You should explore each of them to see which one fits your situation the best. In general this is how they work:

- you and the seller set up an automatic payment system from your banks through the website
- your rent payment gets automatically deducted from your account and deposited into your seller's account
- the website you use processes and logs that payment
- that website then reports your payment to RentBureau which shows up on your Experian credit report
- As you continue to use the service you create a positive rental payment history. which helps your credit score

Without the benefit of experience I cannot recommend one over another, but I do recommend that you ask your seller to use one of these services. If you are rebuilding your credit pile on the positives. A history of making on-time payments in the exact home you are trying to buy should be a big help when a lender is reviewing your credit history.

Chapter Checklist:

___The first thing is to not give up hope. Just believe that it will get better and this will help you change your mind set.

___Next, start taking action! This means taking those first few difficult steps of answering those debt calls (if you have them) and starting to keep track of who is asking for what and why.

___Set a goal to make it better based on your timeline to your purchase date and work every day to stay on track. Use your home as your motivation because without good credit, closing the deal on your home will be nearly impossible.

___Live within your means. It is okay to say "I cannot afford it" to things you want so you can save to afford your home.

___Get a free credit report and as much information as you can to get started.

___Gather up all of your bills and calculate exactly how much you have to pay each month.

___Consider your total monthly bills in your budget and adjust accordingly.

___Contact your bank or credit union to see if they have financial advisers who will pull a detailed credit report and go over everything you will have to do to get it on track. Our credit union did this for us for free.

___Write a letter explaining why each debt is there and how you have or will pay it off.

___Make a plan for how you will budget and pay off each and every negative and stick to that plan.

___Look into debt counselors and consolidation services, but avoid those who claim an easy or quick fix. Ask you bank or credit union about the service you are considering before proceeding. They may offer a similar service, or can point you in a positive direction.

___Focus on the positive. Everyone else will be focusing on your negative credit rating. Let them have that. You stay focused and work hard to fix it. A future with good enough credit to close your rent-toown deal is worth the effort. Do not give up.

___Ask seller to set up an automatic rent payment through one of the websites Clearnow.com, Williampaid.com, Renttrack.com or Payyourrent.com so that your on time rent payments get reflected on at least one of your credit reports.

"Good fortune happens when opportunity meets with planning."

Thomas Edison

PLAN B

Contingency plans are key to every plan of action. That was no different in our case. I always called it our "Plan B". It made the calculated risk of renting-to-own feel much safer. Anytime fear of failing to close on our home crept into my mind, I had the security of our plan B to remind me it was going to be okay no matter what happened.

With that said I must impress upon you how important it is to believe in yourself, and your plan, and to not give up. I still believe that is the main reason we were able to pull this whole rent-to-own plan off. Things that are out of our control really did happen from time to time, but we are still homeowners now. Do not trick yourself into believing that the home you found and are living in is your only option to own a home. The more you think that, the more you will believe it, so establish an alternate plan that you are confident in should you fall short on your rent-to-own home. This alternate plan should include a list of worst-case scenarios and how you plan to handle each of them should they occur. Do this early and understand that it will always help to keep you in a "fail forward" mindset. Bad things can and will happen. It is okay to fall short. If it feels like a total life failure to you, that is okay too. It is such a large investment in time and effort that it makes letting go very difficult. Living in a place can create a personal sentimental attachment that can make missing out feel even more devastating. When any of those things happen you do not have to worry because you will have a plan B. Even if you lose your job, it is not as devastating as you imagine it to be.

Think about it this way: you have a savings of a few dollars and know that you can save when you have an income. You have paid off your credit cards, started using them responsibly, or stopped using them altogether. You have begun to or have rehabilitated your credit. You have found a home and established a history of paying a mortgage on time month after month. You are set up better than when you started and are much closer to your goal of home ownership.

Having a backup plan is important because no matter what happens it allows you the ability to "fail forward". We made a "mother-in-law" style apartment in our basement and rented it to a friend, which provided us with a monthly financial cushion, and we talked about taking on an additional roommate if we found ourselves in financial distress. My back up plan was to take the significant savings that we had building and continue to add to it or sit on it if I were to lose my job, learn to live lean on whatever unemployment check I could get and carry on paying the rent on time every month. It might take an additional two years of employment history at my next job, but I was in my home with an open-ended lease option to buy so there really was not as much of an urgency to close the deal. But this may not be the case for you. Most sellers take advantage of the typical "two year time limit clause" that is written into some rent-to-own agreements, and if you enter into that contract, be aware that you will need to plan to let go of your home, dream, and option money should you fail to receive financing before the contract expires.

Shop around for an open-ended rent-to-own agreement or negotiate for one if you can. Two years just isn't long enough to improve your credit to the magic number for most people (and, as we learned during our two years, the magic number for credit worthiness changes constantly). This is another reason why a plan B is so important. Our plan B was to become FHA eligible: If we had to wait two more years and did not get our lease option home we would have savings left over after we made an FHA down payment on another one. I could pay down my student loans and the home loan much faster and keep a savings. I recognized that no matter what the outcome, I was saving the current homeowner from foreclosure, and I was going to finally have home-buying power that I did not have when I started my rent-to-own journey. It was a win-win even if I did not ultimately buy the home. A rent-to-own experience can be a very good even if you do not get your home. If you make mostly good decisions as you go you will set yourself up to be well down the path to home-ownership, and you can and should try again. Nobody is perfect, so do not feel like one bad mistake will trip you up. It is a true journey with a defined end point that is likely to take years, so you have plenty to time to right the ship and stay on course. Each day that you keep your savings where it is or add to it, you are moving forward.

At any point in our plan B if we found ourselves with still improving credit, and our savings in tact, we could start immediately shopping around for FHA eligible homes. It would mean moving if we found something, but if you continue to move forward in the face of challenges you often find new and even better opportunities. If you are sitting back feeling bad about your situation other people with be finding those opportunities. Be ready for anything. Have a backup plan you feel good about. Be ready for unexpected obstacles. Take them as challenges. Be creative and smart when thinking about finding solutions.

Remember that it is important to use your rentto-own plan as the overall plan to improve your credit. This is also a key component in creating your backup plan. Being thrown off your plan for your rent-to-own can be devastating to your credit if you fail to make rehabilitating and improving your credit a part of your backup plan. They have to be in conjunction with each other just the same as the plan you make to get your rent-to-own home. You will not be successful at closing the deal on any home if you do not meet certain credit requirements. Our backup plan allowed for us to afford to live on an unemployment check. It also allowed us to afford to live and still afford our house even if we had to take a pay cut. Because of this, we were confident that we could hold the line on our savings, and our credit, if we ran across a major obstacle in our rent-to-own journey.

If you follow that advice you will be able to have a solid base to build your backup plan. If you are unable to attain your rent-to-own home, and it can happen for many reasons, remind yourself of the security provided to you in your plan B. Even if you do everything right there are events that can happen out of your control that can cost you your rent-toown home. It is not the end of the world if you are able to improve your credit along the way with a growing savings and a steady budget. You could end up shopping for a FHA home instead of a rental for your next residence.

Make your plan to get your rent-to-own home and then make a plan to finish far ahead of where you started. This way your road to home ownership continues forward even if you end up going down a more traditional path.

We made a number of attempts to close the deal on our home between October 2013 and July 2014. After the 5th attempt resulted in yet another failure, we decided to give up. The stress of trying and failing the 5th time after accomplishing so much in turning our credit around and saving and raising money was too much when coupled with other life stresses. Our relationship was stressed and uncomfortable. It spilled over into our professional lives and we began to wonder why we were working so hard to be continually told that we were denied a loan for a home we had proven we could afford.

We chose to go through this home purchase without an agent representing us. We were willing to learn what we had to in order to save the money, something like $6,000+ according to Sean Stolte, the amazing real estate agent we met with. While we learned enough to negotiate and advocate for ourselves with the bank, that is were our real estate agent skill ended. That decision not to use an agent almost proved to be the road block that cost us our home. Without an agent the bank did not communicate any of the mortgage terms to us or the seller until it went to escrow. For example, on 4th attempt to close the bank put the wrong down payment amount on our paperwork for both us and the seller. Somehow they had him paying nearly $10,000 out of his pocket to close the deal. He was irate and we did not blame him. He told everyone that the deal was off. He assumed because we did not mention any of this to him, we were somehow complicit in crafting those numbers. We were not. The bank also had us contributing well over$50,000 in total down payment. We were short of that number too. It looked like the deal was off. We were crushed.

In the depressing days that followed we had to go back and review our plan B. It worked. We had both improved our credit well into the range necessary to buy a home. We had a huge savings account (huge for us) that we could use to buy any home we liked in our price range. We had all of the necessary paperwork organized and ready to go. If we hit the market actively looking for a home we were in a position to be as competitive as anyone. All this after being laughed out of the mortgage broker's office 2 1/2 years earlier. We actually felt pretty good about our situation. If we had never made this plan B early on and accepted that we might fail, we might have lost everything in that one moment of despair. I should point out that after the failed 5th attempt to close we started shopping around for homes in our price range. This was not something that we did often as we loved our house and were happy there. What we found was that while we were in a position to hit the market we were now priced out of the Seattle market. We would have had to look at homes in neighboring towns in order to execute our plan B. We did not anticipate this drastic change in the market when we made our backup plan.

Staying focused on our goal and working as hard as we could to close the deal really put us square into the bull's eye of our plan B, and when the seemingly disastrous situation struck it only took a day or two of me feeling sorry for myself before I realized that we could achieve our plan B. No matter what, that was a goal that only we could fail to reach, so we knew we were going to be okay. In fact, it was almost exciting to think about the other homes on the market that we might find. We started to shop around when we found out that our old mortgage banker, Michael Press, moved to a new bank and was back on our case. Plan B was there for us because we were prepared with it. Thankfully this story ends with us getting our rent-to-own home, but if not I am confident that having a plan B would have had us in another home we loved just as much. It would have almost definitely been a lesser investment and not in Seattle, but at least we were in a position to jump right back into the local real estate market.

Chapter Checklist:

___Draft at least one back-up plan to your rent-toown home, and be as detailed as you can.

___Add all of your worst-case scenarios to your plan and make a plan to turn each of them into a way to move forward on your path to home ownership.

___Add your back-up plan to your rent-to-own file.

___Remember that when things go wrong they could be a lot worse if you were not prepared with a solid plan B.

___Take this step seriously as it could be your plan B that gets you into your first home.

Happiness is not something
ready-made. It comes from your
own actions."

The Dalai Lama

BE HAPPY

Now that you know what you can afford, and you have
lowered your debts to a manageable level, your credit is on
track to improve and you already have a savings account
that is building by the week, you probably feel like you are
ready to start looking for a home. I say stop right there.
There is no rush. Take some time to get to know places
in a whole new way first. If you do this you can greatly
improve your odds of finding a home in a place where you
will be truly happy, and if you are truly happy your chances of closing on your home are far greater. This is because
you will be more likely to struggle through the difficult
times if you truly love your home and the community in
which you live.

You should not skip this step. I am going to give
you a crash-course on location analysis and business geography that will empower you in the real estate marketplace. Throwing a dart at a map, ordering travel brochures
or simply matching searches by price and amenities is a
risky way to look for homes I have talked about taking cal-

culated risks, and this section helps with the most important risk of all, not sacrificing what makes you truly happy for a rent-toown opportunity just because you happened to find one.

If you had a lot of money and you hired a real estate market analyst they would look at computer software that tells them where you are likely to be the most happy. How in the world can computer software predict or even know where I will be happy? Computers do this by processing lots of data for lots of people. I am going to give you a quick run down of how this works, plus a valuable new perspective on finding a new geography. Keep in mind that it will not make you a real estate analyst. I went through a graduate program as an undergraduate to get this level of education. You would have to invest years of study to really master this concept. However, by simply understanding that happiness is not random and that you can actually go out and find it, you will be far more likely to find a home that will make you truly happy. As difficult as closing a rent-to-own deal is, living in a home that makes you truly happy will help you fight through the most difficult times. Otherwise it is too easy to say, "we did not really want to live here anyway," and give up on the house in which you've already invested so much.

There is a sort of recipe for happiness as it relates to geography. I kind of think of it like making a soup. I am not going to lean too heavily on this soup metaphor, but I will use it to illustrate a few points so you get a picture of how one makes their own happiness. In most soups there are a whole lot of ingredients that, when added together proportionally, work really well to create a delicious meal. Keep that simple metaphor in mind.

Think of it as sourcing data from all over the world and putting it into one place, a computer, just as you would source the ingredients for your favorite soup and put them into a heated pot. Without a good soup or stock pot you just have a wet pile of raw veggies and meats. Not much you can do with that, and without a powerful computer and software there is not a lot you could do with mountains of data.

Here is how this data is compiled and tracked. First you (the consumer) go shopping. At checkout you use a plastic card of some kind to pay. Every transaction like that is databased and tracked. All of that data and tracking gets stored on a computer at a company that specializes in consumer data collection, storage, analysis and distribution. If you are old enough to remember back before bank cards you will remember that they used to have to ask you for your zip code at the check-out in order to attach it to your consumer data. Now it is all digital and automated and more accurate as they use zip + 4 codes rather than the more general five digit zip codes. The zip +4 codes allow them to attach your data to a specific house in a location rather than be represented as a piece of a general area. That data alone is very powerful for marketers and businesses, but it falls a little short of telling you where you will be happiest. To fit this into our soup analogy think of consumer data as the "meat" in our soup. It is so important to the final dish that the base of the soup, its stock, is derived from the simmering meat. Without this critical ingredient your soup will have trouble coming together at all.

Next, there is another computer holding public record information. Some of this comes from the census survey you take once every 10 years, but there is still a lot more information collected by the IRS, your local and state governments and so on. Other information is data that reflects where actual physical items on the landscape are located like water, land, streets, buildings, landmarks and homes. All of that information is stored on other computers but unlike consumer data much of that data is available for free. In our happiness soup this is the veggies. All kinds of free data is out there for you. You can add as much in as you find relevant to your life. Housing values, median income, local schools, age, transit or highway access, crime rates, graduation rates, voting patterns, etc are all factors you can and should consider. There is so much of this data out there for free you can spend days and days analyzing what factors make you most happy. These "veggies" are not as important to the soup as the meat which makes the stock, but they add important color, flavor, and nutrition and should not be ignored. You can choose the ones you need or like and forget those that you do not.

As this data gets renewed and refreshed with

more up-to-date and accurate stats, often old data is added to this data equation in order to understand changes in human behavior such as where and why people seem to be moving to one place or another. Consider this old data the "leftovers". You should probably use it up rather than throw it out. While it may not be oven-fresh anymore, it is still okay to eat and could really help your soup. Often I can find the older data for free, and usually it's more than enough information for making the basic decisions about my personal geography and happiness. If all you can find is older free data, use it. It is still better than throwing a dart at a map, and I have made some good soups from nothing but leftovers.

Now armed with mountains of data, analysts compile this into one computer that is equipped with powerful mapping software often call geographic information systems (GIS). They layer all of this data on a map and patterns of all kinds of human behaviors start to emerge in different geographies. Some of these patterns include whether or not you go out to eat or cook, watch TV or read, prefer hip hop or urban country, have health problems or work out, are young or old, etc. Crunching data with GIS is not unlike layering all of your soup ingredients into a large pot that heats, stirs and simmers your soup for you. By adding in all of the factors that make you happy and cross referencing them on a map you will see that there are places out there that fit you very well. It is in those places, where there are a lot of other people just like you, who enjoy many of the same things you enjoy, in which you will greatly increase your odds of finding a community and home that brings you real happiness. It sounds like a simple premise at the end: if there are a lot of people just like you around, they will create restaurants and businesses that you like as well. The neighborhood will feel like it was waiting there for you all of your life. There will be other places on the map in which there is little to no one like you. You will likely not feel as happy in those areas. Identifying the places with the most things that make you happy is like tasting a soup filled with all of the things that you like and finding out that it is delicious.

You would not just randomly grab things around your refrigerator/freezer, throw them into a pot and call it a soup. That is just like throwing a dart at a map and exclaiming that you are moving where it lands expecting to be happy with that decision when you arrive. That soup may not taste quite right. There are specific ratios of ingredients that you like that come together just right to make it all work best for you. Data can help you create or more accurately find those communities full of the ingredients necessary for your happiness.

I do not expect you to purchase and learn expensive GIS software or terabytes of data, though you can, and it is far more affordable now than it was even when we started our home search. ESRI offers all kinds of classes on the subject as well as user friendly online GIS tools. We were on a very tight budget so I used free resources, supplemented them with my knowledge of the subject, was confident in my ability, and it worked. You can learn to use some of these tricks, and you should. It is a powerful perspective on places and will empower you in the real estate market. Business are often more in tune with how powerful this data is, but sometimes people notice these patterns on their own as well. These business principles will help you because just like a business uses GIS and data to make good financial decisions, you can do the same with your investment in your rent-to-own home. It just takes diving into the data and keeping an open mind about yourself and what patterns of behavior are most common to your life.

A friend of my wife has a unique, albeit unorthodox, way of looking for new neighborhoods to live in, but she is on to something. She is a Volkswagen driver. She loves their cars and has always had a lot of luck with them. Over the years she has noticed that the places where she has been most happy there seemed to be a lot of Volkswagens driving around. She remembers seeing them in driveways and passing up and down her street all of the time. Keeping this in mind, when it is time to change her geography she starts by searching the classified ads for new rentals. She then goes out to visit the neighborhoods. She is looking for a lot of factors that would make her happy, but she ultimately makes her decision based on whether or not she sees a lot of other Volkswagens in the driveways. She is actually performing a form of real estate market analysis using consumer behavior observations. By looking for patterns in the cars sitting in driveways and those driving by, she is observing consumer behavior patterns to see if there are a lot of people who are similar to her. Consumer behavior can be used to accurately predict a lot of other human behavior and is an important part of demographic data as well as real estate market analysis. There is a good reason why this has worked so well for her, and it is because those behavior patterns really do matter. Volkswagens are large and hard to hide so my wife's friend sees them easily. What is not in clear view are all of the other similarities that are not visible to the naked eye.

It never occurred to me to think about any of this location decision-making from the perspective of what cars people drove. Rather this was presented to me in my studies in terms of business location analysis. Businesses that utilize lots of data to locate their operations can enjoy the benefit of wise choices.

Choosing wisely for a business is measured in profits or money saved. In order to understand how location analysis evolved into what it is today, my college classes examined the subject in terms of business geography and we began with Johann Von Thunen way back in the 17th century. Von Thunen was the first person to observe that different industries were located in certain parts of the landscape based on where they originated from (crops in the field) to where they had to end up (in town at markets).

From Von Thunen we looked at Jack Kilmartin,

CEO of Mervyns, who used to track the cars that parked at his stores to their driveways, mapped out addresses, and realized that information about customer geography (where they lived and shopped) was what he needed to understand the best place to open another store to reach those customers who were just too far out to be regular shoppers. That type of smart thinking solved a problem for the customers who lived too far from his Mervyns store because he now knew exactly what neighborhood to open a new store in to reach the maximum amount of customers in the new neighborhood.

Blockbuster Video, back before the internet got fast and accessible, used a similar technique to Kilmartin's, but this time with GPS and GIS tools. Blockbuster used these to find the best neighborhoods and specific blocks in those neighborhoods to open their new stores. It worked, and for a time Blockbuster Video was the big provider of movies once they were out on video. Blockbuster used business geography (think soup) to make great location decisions because they found all of the neighborhoods with the most video watchers packed into specific geographies. Then they opened up new stores directly in those neighborhoods. By doing so they made a stop at Blockbuster the basis for a night of family entertainment in towns across America. Even if the locally owned video store was the only game in town, if they had chosen a location on a hunch (likely in a Main Street area) compared to Blockbuster's analysis Main Street was often a poor location and Blockbuster simply put them out of business.

They beat them by identifying the best location in town and opening up as close to that spot (or spots) as possible.

Understanding how businesses use location analysis really helped me apply that type of thinking and analysis to making a good rent-to-own decision. As you can tell, we thoroughly examined the topic and because of that background I was able to apply business geography to shopping for a home.

You've probably heard the saying "location, location, location" as the key to real estate, and if you have then you already understand the basis of real estate market analysis, and you understand why I am emphasizing this point. To start thinking about real estate market analysis in a deeper way you have to think about the saying "birds of a feather flock together." That saying in this context is meant to represent the people who reside in those locations, locations, locations. A perfect location for me may be much different than a perfect location for you. If we have the same idea of what a perfect location is, then we likely have a lot of other things in common as well. Where a place is, is really just its geography.

Who inhabits that geography is that place's demographics, and demographics are what makes a place what it is in the world because we only have our own human experience to measure the world by. It is just as important as the physical geography of a place, if not more important. That is why all of these location analysis examples worked, because all real estate does come down to the location and who lives there.

My wife's friend observed one tiny pattern statistically speaking, but cars are large and hard to hide away so she noticed a lot of Volkswagens where she was happiest. If she would have had access to the same demographic data that Blockbuster Video had, she would have noticed a lot of other patterns in addition to the Volkswagens, and she may have been able to discover the exact block and even house in which she would be most happy in those Volkswagen-laden neighborhoods. If she were using that demographic data those neighborhoods would have population segments attached to them that represent the similar groups of people who live there. This makes it much easier to track and understand consumer patterns. Names for these groups of people often represent their interests. Claritas, who has a very helpful free online demo of their demographic data, defines groups by their similarities and names them accordingly. Here are some examples of names of segmentations of people: "Movers and Shakers", "God's Country", "Urban Achievers", "Suburban Sprawl", and "New Homesteaders". If this is starting to sound completely foreign, that is okay. Once you familiarize yourself with the Claritas system, its labels will help you know where you best fit in.

If I am going to truly represent our journey to home ownership I feel I have to be upfront about my passion for population demographics and my education in real estate market analysis and city planning. I need to introduce you to the same free tools that I used and offer you a general understanding of how to use them. I was able to search for houses in very specific neighborhoods in which I knew I could afford the homes and in which I knew I would be truly happy. That is a big advantage when searching for a needle in a haystack. We found our rent-to-own home with our first lead! That may be unusual, but it is not an accident or simply luck. It began with making every decision and risk a calculated one.

When I was younger I became somewhat obsessed with cities. We lived far out in rural Pennsylvania, and when we had an opportunity to travel I would fall in love with nearly every new city we would explore. What struck me most about them was how different the feel was. Everything from the energy to the cuisine to the architecture to the way people get around to the different cultures of people who live in each place. It was recommended to me that I study demographics, so I did. I memorized the populations of the largest 100 US cities and, as if that was not enough, I would memorize all of the demographic data in the World Almanac as well. It was a strange obsession, but I loved it, and it taught me a lot about places and people. As I got older and traveled I understood a lot more about why places differed from one another and could focus in on getting to know them on a deeper level.

I was fortunate to find business geography as a course of study to give me the ability to take that passion for places to a much deeper understanding and the ability to apply it to a myriad of opportunities in the real world. I am also fortunate that I chose to apply it to shopping for a rent-to-own home in Seattle. I used all of the available and often free demographic data to make our rent-to-own home a calculated risk rather an just a risk.

None of this is a new idea. You may already use this type of data to market your small or large business. Whether you do or not, I want to get you to look at that data through the lens of who you are, or to put that in demographic terms, which segmentation profile you fall into. Now armed with your budget you can start to search for geographic areas that have homes you can afford and a lot of other people with similar interests and lifestyles to you. For those of you who do not already have access to this data I am going to show you a couple of places I used to narrow my searches down to find our perfect home.

I started with hometownlocator.com. This is an excellent free website that I have used for years. It outlines the general demographic data (think soup veggies) of any city or town you search for. It also links to a ton of other helpful resources. Spend time on this site (hours if necessary) comparing a place's demographic data and you will start to notice all sorts of interesting things about places like home prices, household incomes, population density, schools, crime, too much to list. There are a lot of sites like this, and I encourage you to find the one you like the best. Wikipedia is a good starting place for most general knowledge inquiries. If you're happy where you currently live, look it up using your zip code. Hometownlocator will give you a statistical snapshot of where you live so you can start to get an idea of the type of data that matches up with your community.

Search for other cities or neighborhoods that you are considering with rent-to-own options. If they look dramatically different in the data, they most likely are. That could mean that you are making a move up to a new place that will make you happy, or it could mean that you will feel out of place and want to leave. In my experience I always ended up feeling a little out of place when I lived in places that were contrary, demographically, to where I was happy.

After doing some searches and seeing patterns of similarities of places and those that are outliers, you can still dig a little deeper. Based on the places you find on hometown locator you should think about looking at them a little deeper. Originally I used ESRI's website to go deeper into my search of neighborhoods. ESRI used to provide a free trial snapshot of their amazing demographic data and mapping software. ESRI is trusted by many businesses, cities, colleges and universities as their source of geographic and data system software. ESRI uses what they call lifestyle segmentation profiles to summarize households based on their demographic data and consumer patterns. This is especially useful in real estate market analysis. As a consumer you have access to more of this powerful data than ever before. Use it. You do not have to be an analyst. You can figure it out by spending some time exploring the maps of people and all of the data about them.

Know your (free) data sources

Normally I would point you in the direction of ESRI's website so I could share the same free demo resource that I used, but it appears as though ESRI has changed their website and no longer provides this demonstration service. It does look as though their product has gotten much better which is not a surprise as they are an outstanding business, but you will have to pay for it, and if you are like us then your budget will trump fancy software. There are lots of companies that compile this data and it is hard to rank one above another as they all do outstanding work. I just happened to have some experience with ESRI so I found myself going back there to reference this data.

I did discover another online software demo that you can use to compare demographic data by zip codes, Claritas. Claritas has the best free demonstration software that I could find on the web and I recommend checking it out. At the time of writing this book, Claritas' demo is free and easy to use. Simply enter the zip codes into the search bar and they will list the demographic profiles within that zip code. You will have to cross reference them with the general explanation of each demographic profile to get a better snapshot of each neighborhood you are considering as you search for a rent-to-own home.

You will be amazed at how the general data they provide for free can give you real insight into a place before you even visit. If the general patterns of the different segmentation profiles of where you are looking to rent-to-own match up with the patterns of the places that make you happy, you are finding where to search for your home.

Now that Hometownlocator.com has oriented you in understanding the data behind real estate markets, and Claritas has allowed you to go much deeper in understanding how all of that general data gets broken down into patterns of behavior and attached to each consumer and their household, and you see some general neighborhoods in which you are confident, you will be happy based on the things that you enjoy. But you need to understand if buying in those zip codes is actually a good investment. That means that it is time to get to know Zillow.com.

I love Zillow.com because they have tons of free data, and they know how to use it to empower the real estate consumer and agent. As I mentioned before, we found our home on Zillow.com, so I will always feel comfortable recommending that others use their website. When I first visited Zillow it was for a much different reason than to find a rent-toown home. It was to make certain that the neighborhoods or zip codes that I was going to search for a home in were showing the kind of trends that gave me confidence to make an investment there. Zillow.com will show you years of market trends, not only for the zip code you are considering, but also for the exact addresses where you find rentto-own homes. This means Zillow will show you the home's value month after month with easy to read graphs and charts. You will see if the value has been steadily increasing or decreasing and how those gobs of demographic statistics (that now have a lot of meaning for you) add up in the actual real estate market. If something you see about your house on Zillow raises red flags, like a sudden drop in value, then you know all of your research is paying off. You will be able to ask important questions about the home. You will be able to avoid jumping blindly into any bad situations.

Zillow will also show you what other houses are selling for in the zip codes you are searching. This, along with market trends, is key information when you are going to negotiate a locked in price. In our case, houses were not really selling at all when we first looked at our home, but almost all of them saw their first increase in value since the housing market crash of 2007. That increase along with all of the other factors that told me I would be happy in this home's zip code gave me the confidence to take the calculated risk of getting locked into a home price during a time of very serious uncertainty.

After closing our rent-to-own deal and visiting Zillow again we saw the incredible equity we made in our home purchase, but we also saw that homes in the neighborhood were now selling quickly, and often for much more than their listed value and asking price. That calculated risk I took was exactly correct. Just as I had expected, the data did not lie.

Zillow.com also lists homes facing foreclosure. This is exactly where we ended up finding our home. If an area has a lot of homes in foreclosure it could be a red flag signaling you to stay away, or it could be more like our case in which you can help someone save their home from repossession. If you are looking to help someone solve their foreclosure problem, you can build a relationship with them that is mutually beneficial and results in incredible outcomes for both parties.

In our case it was obvious that the Seattle market would rebound as our diverse economy showed little signs of slowing down through the economic downturn. Giants like Amazon were hiring steadily in Seattle in early 2008. They do not have a lot of low wage jobs at Amazon.com, so there was a steady stream of people moving here who could afford a home and who could afford to wait until the market rebounded before shopping for a home. There were also cranes all over Seattle during the downturn. I recall people asking, how they could be building so many condos while the market could not support it? The answer is simple: those contractors hired real estate market analysts who crunched all of the data and said, "It is safe for you to build. You will see a return on your investment." There was also massive investment in infrastructure going on in Seattle all throughout the downturn. Sound Transit, the regional transit board, was moving forward on a light rail project which has been successful. Cities investing in high density residential development, transit and infrastructure projects, and with diverse high tech economies, are growing cities, and in general those are signs that home ownership is likely to be a good long term investment.

This is because when you see all of these things going on concurrently in a city, that city is growing and planning for a lot more growth. I saw those same signs and never doubted that the economy here was headed in the right direction. If you see signs of life like this where you live and you balance that with some good research it will help to tip you off that you are likely making a good long-term investment.

If the opposite is true then you might want to dig a little deeper before committing to spend a lot of money on a home. The opposite can look like crumbling infrastructure, unfunded transit, vacant lots, condemned housing, suburban flight, population loss, falling home prices, economic inequality and political instability. Keep an eye out for these signs, and do a lot of research. When you are talking about what could be the biggest investment in your life, you can't do enough research before making your decision. Remember to make calculated risks.

This is a lot of data to sit down and learn how to sift through, but it is worth it. Go slow and invest some real time in creating a better understanding of real estate markets, how you fit into them, and which ones will pay off for you in both happiness and equity. If you are happy every day while renting your home, you will be far more likely to stay on track, save money, rehab your credit and close the deal. Happiness was really the key factor in our success, and it could likely help propel you to success as well. Poor credit for whatever reason is a very high hurdle to get over. It was our single biggest hurdle. We often wondered if we could improve our credit in time to close. You may face similar doubt that you can reach your goal. If, like us, you are truly happy where you are, you will fight through that doubt until the end when you close. For me, the happiness of my family trumped all else.

I also believe that utilizing tools like these can make a difference in the bank's willingness to give a loan. In our case we found a fantastic deal which seemed like much less of a risk for them as well: if we ended up foreclosing on the home they could quickly turn around and sell for a big profit. If you find a deal that looks like the price is much higher than what other homes are selling for, you might want to stay away. Why would a bank want to loan you far more than what the home is actually worth? If they see you are making a good investment in yourself and your future, you can help to give an underwriter the confidence that you found a good investment for them as well.

Using data can also help you identify real estate trends in areas where you are looking to rent-to-own. Right now in Seattle there are very few single family homes on the market that we could afford. Condos however are still in some abundance, and not a bad option to start with if you are looking to own rather than rent. Especially for young professionals or anyone who prefers not to have to do yard work and general maintenance. Prices here are still relatively good and options are still available. Be creative with your search and do your best to use all of the tools you have to make the best investment decision you can. The more reasons you can give yourself to be motivated to close the deal, the better your odds. We did not search or try to attain a condo through a rent-to-own but if you are a condo type of person then I encourage you to try. If where you are is anything like Seattle, then the condo market is a much better starter-home market.

Using information will empower you as a buyer

Now let's get back to the old saying, Location, location, location. Location matters. If you start to think of places in terms of data/statistics and use the the tools I've outlined here and the hundreds of others, you will find that you are capable of making very good decisions or calculated risks about which neighborhoods to search for your home. Should you find yourself able to move around the country, you open up a lot of other options to find happiness as well as more rent-to-own potential and much better prices.

Once you get comfortable with all of the demographic data and how to look for commonalities and patterns that match the places that make you happy, you can scale that search out to look for different cities and even regions of the country that might make you happiest.

I knew pretty early on in my study of demographics and cities that Northern California to the Pacific Northwest fit my demographic profile better than any other region of the US. There are pockets of places around the US that are very fitting for me and I have lived in some of those places and enjoyed my time there. I always felt kind of compelled to at least experience the place that had the most places and opportunities for me to be happy, and as a result I was always willing to move about and try new places. It was a great decision. Now that I am living in Seattle, I no longer find myself thinking about a better place. It works to know what makes you happy because now it can give you a much better idea where you will be happy.

It can also help you find a place that you can both be happy with and afford. If I did not arrive in Seattle at the lowest point of the housing depression, I may have found myself looking at other cities in the West and Northwest to find a rent-to-own home. There are other cities that I would be happy living in. Portland is one of the best cities in the US. It has demographic influences from both Seattle and San Francisco. I know I would be happy living in Portland. While Portland is not a cheap city to live in, it is more affordable than Seattle and much more so than San Francisco. My study of demographics and my brief (and unhappy) experiment living in the suburbs of Philadelphia taught me that I am not a suburbanite. I know that I do not find happiness in the burbs, so moving to another urban area would be my best bet to land a home that would make me happy. If you are not able to make a big move in order to find your home, it may take you a little longer, but do not sacrifice what makes you happy. Know where your best neighborhoods and communities are and really work hard to find a home in those places.

There are different regions of the country that fit me well too. They are just not as good a fit as Seattle. Denver, Boston, New York, and San Francisco are close matches but also very expensive. Cleveland, Milwaukee, Detroit, Baltimore, Philadelphia, and Pittsburgh are cities that have good demographic matches for me. They have varying levels of affordability, but in general they are not considered expensive cities. Cleveland and Detroit are very affordable right now, but while affordable are they good investments? With improving credit and manageable debt one could work a modest job and still save up enough for a sizable percentage of a down payment on a home in one of these cities. For instance, a $45,000 home would need a $9000 down payment to put 20% down.

20% down on your home gives you some freedom to work with low but improving credit and some manageable debt. Financing $36,000 also makes your monthly mortgage payment a fraction of what it would be in a city like Seattle.

You have to really study housing values and see how they are trending in those places. If they are trending down, be wary of locking into a long-term lease. Or negotiate a realistic price based on the market trends and go for it! There are towns in the county I grew up in Central Pennsylvania in which one can purchase a livable home for $5,000. These are good affordable homes located in nice quiet communities. The problem is that those homes have lost most of their value and there is little sign that they will ever gain any value back. In fact, they may continue to lose value. Even if you only invest$5,000 in a first home and pay it off right away, if that home loses value then, yes, you have a place to live, but you did not make a good investment as that home has cost you in lost equity. Be very careful to make a sound investment decision. Do not buy a home simply because you can. With that said, if you live in a small town in Central Pennsylvania's coal hills and you find an inexpensive rent-to-own home and you are confident that you will be happy in that community, then make the deal. Investing in your happiness will set you up for a nicer life regardless if you made a good investment or not.

Once you know the data and how you fit into it you will start to see possibilities all over the U.S. Throwing a dart at a map or reading travel information about places to decide where to live is as random as your accuracy or how much a place's city council spent on marketing. Make informed decisions when you are thinking about an investment as big as a house.

This is a complex topic, but there are resources

on how to use demographic or marketing segmentation profiles on our website, rent2ownbook.com. We will help you learn your own marketing segment and how it can help you identify places in which you will fit right in and find happiness. You can also look at those segments that you desire to see what type of job and education you will need in order to get into a neighborhood that you want.

Chapter Checklist:

___Do not throw a dart at a map or read travel brochures or tourism websites.

___Visit Hometownlocator.com and study the demographics of the place you currently live, then review the places that you think you want to live—identify the statistical similarities and statistical differences.

___Visit Claritas' website and review their free demographic demo and the explanations of the different population segmentations. Study how all of that demographic information you saw at hometownlocator.com gets used with consumer data to identify patterns of human behavior across a geographic landscape organized by zip codes.

___Find the segments on Claritas' list with explanations that best reflect who you are and want to be and begin searching for those places.

___Visit Zillow.com and then review the zip codes that you believe represent the places and population behaviors that make you the most happy. Look for what would make one place a better investment than another and try to understand why that is. Look for trends in housing values and market sales.

___If you are still confused or more so after reading this, talk it over with someone you know in real estate. Sometimes another perspective really helps illuminate a complex subject.

___Repeat these steps when you actually begin reviewing the lists of rent-to-own homes that you find.

FINDING A RENT-TO-OWN HOME

It can be difficult to find rent-to-own homes. You simply will not find many trustworthy listings. You may not find any at all depending on where you live and what the market is like. Do not be discouraged. The internet resources from Chapter Six made it relatively easy for us to find our home and should be a big help for you as well.

Most Important Step: Avoid Rent-to-Own Scams

Just because we had a lot of success through our rent-to-own purchase does not mean that all rent-toown agreements are equally safe. In fact, most rentto-owns fail because people create scams around them to rig the game in their favor. They can do this because many renters decide they want to own a home before they start fixing their credit or saving money, which creates a demand for rent-to-own homes from people who are not quite ready for home ownership. That is why the rent-to-own space has been filled with so many shady business people. It is hard for me to imagine starting a business like this, but many people see this as an opportunity to take advantage of people who they see as inevitable failures anyway, so they might as well get what they can before the renter loses all of their savings to someone else. It is a sad fact of rent-to-own homes and a big part of the reason the rent-to-own home reputation is so poor.

There are no shortcuts to home buying whether it is a rent-to-own or not. Because of this, there are no shortages of rent-to-own scams pretending to make it easy to get you into a home. I have posted examples of alleged scams on Rent2OwnBook.com; visit to read what other renters have gone through and see which types of businesses to avoid.

Who are the Scammers?
There are three common types of rent-to-own scams to avoid:
1. Third party businesses (mostly online) that want money up front to get you in a house, or worse yet, just to see houses.
2.Bad landlords who use rent-toown offers to collect more money from renters but have no real intention of selling the home.
3. Real estate investors who will buy a home you want and then offer to sell it to you as a rent-to-own deal.

Scam 1: Third Party Businesses (often online)

Do not pay anything up front to anyone. Rentto-own businesses often employ some good sales people who will pressure you into paying a lot money so they can put you in a home. They will tell you there is one home ready to go and a lot of other people are looking at it. Their tactic is to create a sense of urgency and scarcity. Once you are afraid to lose the home, they expect you to give them money. It is common for the renter to fork over hundreds or even thousands of dollars and then not even get a call back. If you do hear back it will often be the message, "that home is gone but I will contact you with others." Then you will get a series of excuses as to why they have not been able to deliver on their promises. They got what they wanted from you, and they do not guarantee that you will get into the house.

Many new online rent-to-own listing services have popped up since we began our search. Use caution when examining these. Often, they are started by a middle-man with little to no real estate experience who sees a "get rich quick" opportunity in a challenging real estate market.

One way to spot a red-flag is to see if they ask you for money just to see properties and/or to be connected to buyers. If you see these, walk away from them. There are a lot of people out there who want to prey upon you because you are likely to be in a more desperate credit situation than a conventional home buyer. If you give them money up front, they have no stake in your success down the line. They got what they wanted from you and more often than not they look down on you because of your credit and expect you to fail anyway. They act like your friend and partner but really look at you as an easy target to fork over money to them that you do not have to give. Remember the savings chapter? You have to be the lock and key on your own savings account.

If you must use a listing service, use one that is not designed as a rent-to-own business. If you find a rent-to-own business, only use them if they take their payment on the back end of the deal after you close on your home. In this arrangement they have incentive to create a business model that is focused on getting you to home ownership rather than on assuming you will fail and taking what they can from you while you have it.

I checked into a couple of these rent-to-own listing service sites and found homes in my West Seattle neighborhood listed for sale or rent that were not for sale at all. One in particular is right on my morning running route, and was for sale last year. These sites were using a common scam that involves using actual real estate listings to look as if they have a big inventory when in reality the listings are old and out of date. Anyone seeing the house might get excited about an amazing rent-to-own opportunity and fork over the $1500 fee only to be told that the home already sold. The detail that the prospective renter is missing is that the home sold over a year ago and they were duped into thinking there was a real opportunity for them.

I did not run into any reputable looking rent-to-own websites in doing my research for this book. Not one, and I based my judgment on whether or not it was a service I would have used. They all want money before getting you into a home. Imagine if car dealerships worked this way: You would look at cars for a $1500 fee or a monthly subscription with no guarantee that you were going to drive home in one. Would you shop at that car dealership? I hope not; they would be making money without selling anything. They would be very happy to make a lot of money while keeping their inventory (if they even had one).

Bad Landlords

We were so lucky to find a good landlord who was serious about selling his home. He was working to solve a pretty major problem in his life: foreclosure. This made him motivated to create a contract that showed us that he was serious about selling his home. It worked. His logic made sense and we trusted him and took his word. Now we are homeowners, and improbable ones at that.

How do you spot a bad landlord over a good one? Bad landlords will not want to use an escrow company to manage payments. They will not like you hiring an inspector. They will not want you using a real estate lawyer. They will demand a short lease of 24 months or less. They will want an option money payment of more than 3%. They will want high premium rental credits and will not offer a guarantee in the contract that those are to be returned to you should you not get the home. They will not offer to drop the agreed upon price of the home should the home should the value drop. They will take a "my way or the highway" attitude and refuse to negotiate any terms. If this is your experience dealing with a prospective seller (who is really just a greedy landlord in disguise) walk away. They are looking for sucker and you do not want to be that person.

Buy, then Rent-to-own Real Estate Investors

Given that an investors' primary concern is making money, these types of situations should give you pause right from the start. In these scenarios the investor will list some rent-to-own homes that are actually for sale or facing foreclosure. They will then tell you that they will buy the home and sell it to you as a rent-to-own home. While this sounds pretty good on its face, consider why this arrangement is a problem.

They will ask for a large deposit. Do not expect to get that back, as this is how they make money on offering to rent-to-own the home. In addition they will more often than not also ask for the option money payment and rental credits. Their intent is to keep all of this money no matter what happens with the house. Then they can continue to offer rent-toowns in the home if you leave, or sell it in the traditional sense. They take very little risk and see you as an easy target to take your money. If possible I advise you to avoid dealing with anyone like this.

I simply avoided any arrangement like this that I found when searching for our home, but a co-worker of mine who was inspired by our rent-to-own experience seriously considered an option like this.

What she found was that the arrangement was completely one-sided toward the investor, so she and her husband gave up their search for a rent-to-own home and waited to try the traditional path to home ownership once they rebuilt their savings and credit.

Try using free internet resources before shelling out valuable savings just to view properties. You already have a much better idea how to use the free internet resources to narrow your search area down to where you will be happy, and many of those resources can also help you find a rent-to-own home and keep your savings intact and growing. If you find a home listed on Zillow.com, you are very likely to find the same home listed on a "fee-to-see" rent-toown website. Zillow's list is as close to comprehensive as you will find.

This warning goes for sellers as well. If the listing service puts a barrier up in front of a renter, a large percentage of potentially great renters will go to a free site, and it will actually make it more difficult for you to find a qualified buyer. Anyone falling for a "fee-to-see" listing service when they should be saving to buy a home might not be the person you want renting your home anyway.

Renting Options

There are others out there who may not need to search to find a rent-to-own home. They may already be in a home they love as a renter, and want to buy it, and the owner might be willing to sell. Maybe you decide that the waiting does not suit your personality and you just go rent your dream home and make a plan to save up enough money to make the owner a serious offer. I want to touch on these first, then look at searching directly for rent-to-owns. I think it will get you thinking creatively about how you can use a lease option agreement as an alternative path to the perfect home for you.

Let's start with a scenario in which you find a rental home that is in one of your target neighborhoods, you love it, and you know you want to buy it, but it is only listed as a rental home. You can talk to the homeowners up front and simply ask them if they are willing to give you the option to buy at the end of the a rental lease. It could be that homeowner wants to sell but it seems like more work than simply renting it out again. It could also be that they have some sentimental attachment to the property, and if you live in it for a while and care for it they will trust you to be the right person to own it after them. If not you can continue searching until you find a home owner who is renting but willing to sell.

You can also find a home that you can afford in a neighborhood that makes you happy, rent it, and make a long-term plan to save and rehab your credit (if it is low). When you are ready to buy, ask the homeowner with no warning. If you come to them with a substantial down payment, pre-approved financing, and a decent offer, they may decide taking the money is worth it to them and decide to sell. Let them know you are a motivated buyer who is working hard to buy a home. Tell them you love their home and it would be your first choice to buy immediately if they would consider selling to you. You will be surprised by the numbers of home owners renting a property who would rather just sell it to the person who is in there and takes great care of the place, especially when faced with cleaning it out and getting it ready for a new renter who may or may not be as good a tenant as you. Some intend to sell it themselves but the work that goes into that simply does not fit into their schedule. By making a serious offer you could be making it easy for them to finally do it.

If you are already in your home and love it and want to buy it, but it is a bit out of your price range, see if the owner would be willing to negotiate a creative rent-to-own contract. Keep it open-ended and find out how much of a down payment you would need to get conventional financing. For instance, you might be able to get financing for $170,000, but the owner is asking a very fair $250,000. That means you will have to come up with a $70,000 down payment in order to make the financing work for you to buy that home. Large sums of money you do not have might seem like a mountain to climb, but if you make a plan that shows it is possible, it will help convince both you and the seller that you are serious.

Homes Facing Foreclosure

Before I even get into this option at all, I have to say that it is important to do this work on your own. Do not use a rent-to-own listing service for searching out homeowners who need help saving their home from foreclosure. Why? Because there are a lot of scams out there in which the website lists homes that they actually have no stake in whatsoever. They use a listing service and they make them seem as if they are listed on their website as rent-to-own homes, but the reality is that they are already foreclosed upon. You pay a large fee or subscription to look at homes only to find out that the homes are not actually rentto-own opportunities. The business gets their money from you, and in most likelihood you never hear from then again. If you do this research on your own then you can directly contact rent-to-own sellers and deal with them, knowing that they are real and so is the home.

Given how well our deal worked out for both us and our seller, one of our focuses is connecting real home owners facing foreclosure with those who, like us, can afford a home but need a chance to get the money saved or their credit in order. For those facing foreclosure, a rent-to-own offers a quick way to save the home from foreclosure or repossession and save a credit score. Getting out from under a bad situation while avoiding a negative credit impact is a victory, especially if it also means a young family or single parent can get their opportunity to own a home and raise their children in a stable middle-class life. This is how we found a rent-to-own home and made it ours. We started with a general Google search for "rent-to-own". We tried a few others, but the actual key words that worked to find the listing for our home were, "rent-to-own home" ("in quotes" but with or without the hyphens). I eventually found our house listed on Zillow.com. That ad popped because the seller was a savvy internet marketer. He included a bunch of key words at the end of his ad, one of which was "rent-to-own". He made his ad rise to the top of the Google haystack that matched our search with the words "rent-to-own."

"Text this number," the ad said. The number itself was coded with written and numeric numbers presumably to get around some rule that one can't post a phone number on the site, so we texted as instructed. It might have seemed shady to some consumers, but I saw a savvy marketer, someone who understood where to find his target demographic and was willing to get creative to get a deal done. It seemed like exactly what we were looking for and worth a serious reply.

It was a brilliant move on our seller's part. As I said, he knew exactly where to find his target demographic, and he found a way to post pertinent information in his ad. He followed up quickly and was willing to move quickly. We had started our savings and credit rehabilitation earlier thinking we could go the traditional route to home ownership, and starting early paid off big-time for us because that savings ended up becoming the initial down payment on our rent-to-own home. It took my credit until the summer of 2014 to round into home buyer shape. Finding our potential dream home happened much faster than we ever expected, so we were still two thousand dollars short on the option money. We knew we found a rare opportunity so Allison moved quickly and found a local micro credit lending agency. She used her old Honda Civic as collateral to borrow the remainder of the down payment, and we came up with all $7,000 just in time to meet the home owner that first weekend.

You are not likely to find a home so quickly. Allison and I were prepared for a marathon search that could take years. At that time we were living in a 500 foot backyard mother-in-law cottage owned by a wonderful family from Southern California. They were nice and caring people who were kind neighbors and friends. They also provided a fenced-in yard, loved our pets and were pet people themselves, so we were in no hurry to leave that situation. We knew our credit needed some serious rehabilitation, and I had just started the rehabilitation process at that point, so the longer it took us to find a rent-to-own home, the closer we would get to being able to buy through more conventional financing, making it more likely we would eventually close the deal.

My plan was to compile a list of homes listed as a rent-to-own possibility in the neighborhoods I identified to provide our highest probability of happiness. Then I was going to cross reference that list with the county's public records to see who the homeowners were for each of the listed homes. At this point I would use the internet to find phone numbers, emails, or Facebook pages for the homeowners in an effort to talk to them. Then it was on to cold calls, emails, and messages inquiring about leasing their home with an option to buy. Given how many of the homes that had rent-to-own potential reflected in the message were also on the list of homes facing foreclosure, and armed with the hindsight of how well our deal worked out for both us and our seller, I could have simply made a list of homes facing foreclosure and pitched the owners on a rent-to-own. I recommend that you try this. Tell them this story. Let them know that it works, and that it is easy to get started and that you have a plan and are ready to move. They may have to sell their home but they are not losing it and there is a significant, potentially life-changing difference.

I found rental homes and ads that said "owner financing available" and "rent-to-own possibility". I called or emailed about those directly through the ads. A few of those were connected to real estate investors who would simply buy the prospective home and then sell it to us in an attempt to cash in on the "Greater Fool" phenomena. They make out on the option money if you cannot purchase the home before the contract expires; they keep the option money and either rent or sell the home to someone else. We were not against this option, not at all given the scarcity of rent-to-own options out there, but too many of those seemed less like a win-win and more like someone trying to take advantage of people in a down economy, so we did not jump at any of those opportunities. I do want to point out that since the time when we were shopping for rent-to-own homes in 2011 and 2012 during the end of the downturn in the housing market here in Seattle, a number of reputable online rent-to-own listing companies have formed. They are helping to create a safer marketplace for lease option consumers than existed when we were searching. You are more likely to find an honest marketplace for lease options now, so do not discount these marketplaces based upon our experience. Explore these and all options as the best deal for you could be found any number of different ways.

We heard back from the owner of our home more quickly than those business services, and he was serious about selling and ready to move fast. He owned 11 homes; under normal circumstances they were some great investments, but at this time he was hit hard by the collapse of the housing market.

Our seller was a lot like us. He was determined to do it his way even though the banks had other ideas. We were lucky to find a hard-working, smart and honest seller. He was quick with follow-up and his real estate investing savvy and his experience helped guide us toward the best deal in the end. He could have given up and exclaimed that he was yet another victim, but rather than feel sorry for himself he took action and outsmarted the banks and gave us the deal of a lifetime while saving his immediate financial future.

I was so impressed with his plan of action and follow-through because he proved that it was not a zero sum game during the housing crisis. It was not as simple as the story the banks told us. They liked us to believe that the people they kicked out of their homes were irresponsible with money or even lied about their income, and because of that it was their fault. If a person invested in real estate because the market was busting loose, who could blame them? They had the ability and were trying to live a good life like everyone else. To the banks, those irresponsible homeowners had made their bed and now they had to look for a new one or be forcibly removed. Our seller knew that was not his story, and he fought to protect his good name and the credit he built for himself. His ability to keep a level head and intense focus in the face of potential personal tragedy was impressive to see. He made a plan to take on the big banks, executed it perfectly, and won. They did not get his home. Rather, he got more than enough money to pay off his loan, kept his good credit, and even made a little money to walk away with. All of that in addition to the rental equity we paid to him over 27 months.

After watching how clever he was to make this deal, I realized that his plan of action could be replicated by many other Americans who own homes and are still living in the housing crisis. If homeowners facing foreclosure could take this page out of our seller's playbook, they too could save their financial futures. At the time of writing this book there are projected to be 1.3 million homes facing foreclosure in America this year. Many of those potential foreclosures are lumped together in a few geographies that are still in the middle of the housing crisis. If there are just a few thousand homeowners who have the go-getter attitude of our seller, they could potentially, one owner at a time, start to curb the housing crisis in those still-suffering markets. The ripple effect could be huge for both the sellers and the first time homebuyers who are still essentially locked out of receiving credit to get their first home.

We want to help connect more homeowners with renters like us who are driven to own a home and are ready to take serious action now. There are a lot of ways to find similar situations to ours. I recall running across a lot of ads that were for homes that were not for sale but facing pending foreclosure. At first I found this confusing in my search because I did not request to see homes that were facing foreclosure, rather I was looking for rent-to-own ads. To my surprise there were a lot of rent-to-own ads for homes facing foreclosure, so this is not a new or foreign concept to some.

I found the most successful searches for both conventional ads and rent-to-own ads came when we stopped looking for great deals and fixer-uppers and and started looking for what truly made us happy. The neighborhood, transit access, schools, parks, square footage, and commute times all fit into what made us happy. My experience with the approach outlined in Chapter Six really made the difference for us. If I thought that I really liked a neighborhood, I looked for houses in that neighborhood. All the while I was keeping a budget in mind and not looking outside of what we could afford. There were many homes in neighborhoods that I loved that were in our budget. I was not a real estate agent, nor was I a house flipper. I did not get caught up looking for big quick turnarounds to make money. I was focused on trying to access one important component of the American dream, home ownership. In my case home ownership punched my ticket from a working poor to a middle class life. I stayed confident that if I kept my goals big enough but realistic as well that I could achieve them all.

Be confident in yourself, but remember why you are so driven to own a home. Years from now with the benefit of this experience you might find yourself flipping homes and closing deals. Not now. Aim for what a first time home buyer with a shaky credit or no credit history can realistically afford. Do not chase impossible scenarios. Remember to take calculated risks. Trust your budget, your plan, and the demographic data, and be patient until you find the right home.

It is very risky to target homes facing foreclosure as the homeowner has to be in a position to prevent foreclosure through regular payment, and you have to trust that they are going to actually apply the payments you make to their mortgage.

One way to ensure that your payment goes to the seller's mortgage, and in part to the down payment savings, is to set up payment through an escrow company. This offers some protection but also will add to the overall cost with transaction fees. I will touch on this option again, but it is an important question to ask up front if you intend to look for homes facing foreclosure.

During our 27 months the foreclosure warnings did not stop coming to our door. A couple of times the homeowner reached out to us and asked us if we were interested in other homes so he could put our home up on the market. From the way it looked to us, the banks never stopped putting pressure on him. We often had the stress of worrying about losing our rent-to-own home because the homeowner was in dire straights. I always trusted that the seller's situation likely looked a lot worse to us than it really was given we knew so little about the situation. My mind often creates a worse situation than what actually exists in the real world, and it was wise to remind myself of that as we progressed. In the end it all worked out just as we drew it up, 27 months earlier, but living in a home facing foreclosure requires a certain kind of risk taker with thicker skin than most. I happen to fit nicely into that demographic.

Take your time and be creative

There are a lot of ways to find a rent-to-own home. Because it is so unconventional, you are not limited by established systems with stake holders and gate keepers who force you to operate in their well entrenched sales funnels. When searching for a rent-to-own home I was only limited by my own creativity and willingness to work hard and not give up. Right from the start during the search, and then all throughout, it was more difficult to go the rent-toown route, but in other respects it was much easier. It could have taken us many years or even decades to buy a home in Seattle had we waited and done it the "easy way". When looking at our home from that perspective it made it easier for us to reach big life goals in a timeline that made sense to us. Had we gotten a home anywhere else I would have been making my next plan to get another in Seattle. It would have taken a lot more time and work. Now that we have accomplished our goal of owning a home here, we are much further down the road on our other life goals as well.

Keep our experience in mind and remember that it will be worth your time and effort to search for the best possible home for you. Take your time and do it right. It may be the biggest investment you will ever make. Don't just look for something that looks like an easy route to home ownership. Taking short cuts early could make it more difficult down the road. You must really trust the seller of the home with your money and future. If you rush in and work with the wrong person, whether that be a landlord or rent-toown business, you could be setting up a painful experience.

New Ways to Find Homes

I recently discovered Rebls, a new start-up here in Seattle that has a completely new way to search for homes. Rebls lets people shop for any home whether it is for sale or not. As shoppers view homes the stats for each home are compiled. The homeowner then, if ever curious can use Rebls to check their property to see how much interest there from prospective buyers shopping around.

This is an exciting new idea that could change how people shop for homes. Our seller got creative with how he used Zillow.com to get his home listed as a rent-to-own and we were creative with how we used internet resources to find our home. Try these new real estate start-ups out for yourself as you find them. See if you can get creative to either list your home or find a rent-to-own home. Rebls was not there for us to use as a resource. It does not mean that it or Trulia.com or some other new real estate start-up will not be your way to find a home. Try them all including the new ones. The nice thing about start-ups is that they are often testing their ideas and your creativity could play right into their development. With our access to information at our fingertips we are only limited by our own creativity when it comes to finding our dream home.

Chapter Checklist:
In order to find a rent-to-own and help someone before they are foreclosed upon, there are a few very easy steps to follow.

First of all, avoid rent-to-own scams:

___Avoid "fee-to-see" listing services. If they want money up front, they have no stake in your success. There are quality free options available.

___Avoid bad landlords. If they stack the deck in their favor, you can bet that they are banking on your failure to close the deal.

___Avoid real estate investors who offer to buy a home, then offer to sell it to you as a rent-to-own.

How to find the good sellers:

_Search for exactly what you want (put "key words" in quotes).

___Search for homes facing foreclosure.

___Search the public record for the homeowner and reach out to them.

___Start or search for a local rent-to-own/land lease meet up group.

___Call as many rentals that fit your search and happiness requirements.

___Ask if those homeowners are interested in selling.

___If they are interested in selling, offer them a land lease option.

___Be picky.

___Do your homework and stick to your analysis:

- know your budget
- know what you can afford
- set goals
- make a plan to achieve your goals
- only search in cities, states, neighborhoods and places that make you happy

___When you find a home, negotiate and see if the seller is willing to give you the time and flexibility to get your credit fixed and build a savings.

___Get creative with how you find the right home for you by finding and using new real estate resources like start-up, Rebls.com who allows you to search for homes that are not yet on the market.

"There is a difference between a
gamble and a calculated risk."

Edmund H. North

FOUND A HOUSE!

Whether you got lucky on your first day of searching or finally found a rent-to-own home after searching for over a year, you found it, and it is a happy and exciting time. If it is in an area that makes you happy, you can afford it, it is in good shape or a manageable project for you and your budget, and looks like an overall good investment, then you have good reason to be happy. It is a good feeling when you have kept a disciplined budget, stuck to it and have saved up for the option money payment and the big move.

If you have made it this far, then the home owner has agreed to sell to you while you rent and live in the house, and you have agreed to the basic terms of the deal, length of lease and payments and price, but you will need a contract. It is your contract that will protect both you and the seller, so make sure that both of you are happy with the terms of the agreement. What you do not need to do is worry about how legal it looks or sounds. If you both agree to it, sign and date exact copies so each party has an original copy and everyone agrees with the terms; then you can feel pretty safe in your deal. I know that for a lot of you that does not sound like a safe way to protect your investment, but that is exactly how we did it.

If you are still not convinced then this is where you get to make an important choice of whether or not to hire a real estate lawyer, and there are pros and cons to that decision. Each aspect of the choice has some risk. You will need to save every penny to close the deal on your new lease option, and legal expertise is not cheap. In our case we knew how expensive Seattle is. We have decent jobs that allow us to afford this market but not without really sticking to a strict budget. Saving is still really hard on our incomes. Paying for a lawyer would have given us a lot of peace of mind about the legitimacy of our contract, especially given the lack of resources and information that was out there when we were researching our options. But we felt like we could create a legally binding contract based on free information we found on the internet, and in our case it turned out to be the right choice.

Our seller came to us with a contract already drawn up with the terms of a deal. It was obviously a legal template printed off of the internet. His terms were much better than what we expected, but we were not going to simply take the first offer either. We knew too little about the house and my experience negotiating prepared me to walk away from any first offer. It might seem scary to walk away from a great offer, especially when it is better than what you were expecting to get, but you need to stay focused on the big picture. In our case that picture was that the seller was close to losing his house, and it needed a major repair to a sewer line, so he simply approached us with an offer which gave us some room to ask for something. Keep in mind that there was no guarantee that the housing market was on a rebound at that time. In his favor, the house was valued at $240,000 based on what we saw on Zillow.com, which was well above his very fair first offer price of $219,700, and our credit put us in no position to simply walk away and go the conventional route to buy a home. Weighing all of those factors we came up with a counteroffer. Allison asked the seller to drop the asking price of the home by the amount of our initial down payment of $7000. Our seller agreed and crossed off the asking amount of $219,700 and hand-wrote $212,700 on the contract. Both parties initialed the changes and we shook hands and signed the deal.

On the following page you'll find the contract we used. As you can see, there really is not much to it. We did not need to know a lot of legalese in order to put it together and negotiate the terms. We found other examples online, so we knew what he brought to us was a legitimate contract. It was that easy. The contract refers to an "Exhibit A", which was just a standard rental agreement; literally everything we needed to make our lease option contract legal fit on this one sheet of paper.

The very simple contract we used addresses the basics. First you have to identify the legal names of the parties involved in the deal. As you can see, our contract does that. It also has to address the term or length of the lease; the owner generously offered us an open-ended term. If you cannot get an open-ended lease try to get a 30 month term with a six month window to close if 30 months passes and you have been pre-approved for a loan but have not yet closed.

Our contract also addresses the amount of rent that we had to pay. It should have been more clear on utilities and taxes, and this is an example of something a lawyer might have caught if he reviewed the contract for us: our contract says the owner is responsible for utilities. Since we weren't expecting this, we paid the utilities for several months before even noticing it, and never discussed the discrepancy with our seller. It's likely he hadn't intended for utilities to be part of the deal either. Either way, our seller held up the important end of the deal, and we were happy with the contract.

We decided against doing an overpay on our rental payment that would have been placed into a savings account to be used as the down payment on the home. This is sometimes referred to as a rent credit. We did this because we had a plan and a budget and an overpay simply didn't fit into our plan. We agreed to full liability for the property as renters which included taking ownership of all appliances and maintenance and repairs. We could have done a better job of accounting for this in our contract as well, but it was clear between the parties when we agreed.

OPTION TO BUY REAL ESTATE

Dated _____ 2012 _____ 1

1. Parties. This Option is between _____ ("Buyer") 2
and Nathanael Williams, a single person _____ ("Seller"). 3

2. Option or Lease Option. This Option is 4

✓ Part of a Lease between the Buyer (as Lessee) and the Seller (as Lessor) dated _____ 5

Default on that Lease constitutes default on this Option 6

Unrelated to any lease between the parties 7

3. Purchase Price. The Purchase Price of the Property shall be **$212,700.00** 8
_____ Dollars (_____) which shall be paid in cash at closing unless 9
otherwise specified in this Option. The following shall be applied to the: ✗ Down Payment Purchase Price 10

All rent paid under the above Lease 11

The dollar amount filled in at Paragraph 5, below 12

✗ Other **$7,000.00** 13

4. Legal Description. The legal description of the Property is In the above Lease Attached ✓ As follows 14
See attached to lease EXHIBIT-A. 15
16

5. Option/Time Limit. In consideration of ✗ The rent and terms of the above Lease, and/or ✗ **$7000.00** 17
paid by Buyer to Seller, Seller grants to Buyer, and Buyer's successors and assigns, the right to buy the 18
Property on or before **ANYTIME** (the "expiration date") without grace or extension of said 19
date. In any event, the expiration date shall occur on the date prior to the expiration of Buyer or Seller's life 20
(whichever occurs later) plus twenty-one years. 21

6. Notice–Exercise of Option. Buyer may exercise this Option only by written notice personally delivered or 22
sent by certified mail, return receipt requested, to Seller at _____ 23
_____ at least 30 days in advance of the expiration date of this option. 24

7. Closing. At least 10 days before the expiration date of this Option, the Buyer shall deposit into escrow with 25
_____ the Closing Agent, all monies and documents necessary to 26
close this transaction on or before the expiration date. Within 5 days of deposit of Buyer's documents and 27
money, Seller shall deposit into escrow with said Closing Agent all documents and money required of the 28
Seller to close this sale. 29

8. Time is of the Essence. Time is of the essence in this Option. In the event that: (a) Buyer shall fail to give 30
notice of exercise of this Option within the time provided herein, or (b) this sale shall fail to close prior to the 31
expiration date through no fault of Seller, or (c) Buyer shall fail to deposit all necessary documents and 32
money into escrow on or before the time required in paragraph 7, above, then this Option and Buyer's 33
privilege to buy the Property shall terminate and Seller shall retain the option payment set forth in paragraph 34
5 above. 35

9. Purchase and Sale Agreement. Buyer and Seller have completed and attached hereto a Purchase and 36
Sale Agreement. If Buyer exercises this Option, Buyer and Seller shall proceed with the transaction 37
according to the terms and conditions set forth in the attached Purchase and Sale Agreement and unless 38
otherwise provided therein, all time periods stated therein shall run from the date Buyer gives Seller notice 39
exercising this Option (e.g., time periods for obtaining financing, inspections, and title review). In the event of 40
conflict between this Option and the attached Purchase and Sale Agreement, this Option shall control 41

Initials BUYER _APM_ DATE _4/2/12_ SELLER _NcW._ DATE _4-7-2012_ 42
BUYER _____ DATE _4/1/2012_ SELLER _____ DATE _____ 43

In addition to defining our rent payment, our contract also covered our first down payment or option money. This goes directly to the seller and is typically 3% of the assessed value of the property. You can find the assessed value of the property at your city or county tax website. Zillow.com also offers an accurate estimate of the property's value.

One aspect of our deal that we completely left out of the contract was that we agreed to cover all closing costs to get financed. Our seller gave us a great deal and part of that was for us to agree to those terms. We did and held up our end, but leaving this off of the contract almost cost us because it was not clear to the bank and the escrow company that our seller was not responsible for any costs. He was angry with us when the escrow company sent out settlement papers with closing costs listed on his end, and I don't blame him. Eventually when we explained what happened we were back on track, but not including this simple clause in the contract almost cost us our home.

You can account for a lot more in a rent-to-own contract as well. Basically if you have a question about it, ask the seller. Do not be afraid to negotiate. You will have to. All good contacts are arrived at through a negotiation between the involved parties. If you feel like something was left out you can always go back and ask to add it in later.

Our seller was so motivated that he also issued a quit claim deed for us. I believe he did this as a gesture of good faith to us as I am still not certain that it held any real legal weight in the transaction. He is a smart man with a lot of real estate savvy and experience, so I trust that it was part of his plan to prevent the bank from taking his home, but this is not something you need to do in your own deal.

In the end to make a contract legal it requires all parties to sign and date it. This is usually the bottom line of the contact. Without ink signatures and dates, the agreement is not legal.

You may or may not have the confidence with contracts to do this without a lawyer. I did, but I worked every day with contracts for years. I was more than happy to draw one up without a lawyer costing us thousands. You may not be in that position, and I urge you to trust your instinct if it is telling you to hire a real estate lawyer. If you do go it on your own, you can use our contract as a guide or follow some general rent-to-own contact guidelines to help protect you.

To Inspect or Not Inspect

You also have to decide whether or not to pay for an inspection up front. If you get an inspector before entering into a contract and she flags a major issue, then you do not even have to worry about negotiating and signing a deal. The decision of whether or not to get an inspection gave me a lot more pause than whether or not to hire a real estate lawyer. We could see some evidence of water damage in our home, but we also saw evidence of its repair. There was some rotting wood around the garage and some moss on the roof which didn't look good. The home had some plywood siding that must have been used to re-place the original weathered boards, and from the looks of it, the plywood was also starting to reach the end of its life cycle. We also found two outlets in the basement (our soon-to-be mother-in-law apartment) that were blown out which is always scary due to the threat of fire. We had concerns but nothing that raised enough of a red flag for us to call in the inspector. We needed every penny and were willing to take some calculated risks.

The free homeowners class we took explained what to look for to find FHA eligibility. We did a little internet research on that topic on our own as well to be certain that we could meet those FHA requirements. FHA loans require much less of a down payment which can take some of the pressure off of the budget. Because of this at the time we were convinced that a FHA loan would be our best bet. We looked the house over well and de-cided that it was in good enough shape to pass an FHA inspection with a little TLC. You may decide differently depending on your situation. In fact, if you do not have a lot of experience with home maintenance or know what to look for in the way of water damage and other red flags, it is well worth hiring an inspector at $500 to $800. While we did need every dollar, with the benefit of hindsight we could have afforded the inspector and probably should have hired someone to look the home over. When we were finally closing the inspectors who did come to see the home were all impressed with our deal. That would have been nice to know before we ever signed the contract, and could have bought us some peace of mind.

It is important to note that a lot of rent-to-own homes are the fixer-upper type of deals. By fixer-upper, I mean major work is needed that requires contractor expertise. If you have those skills then you are lucky because you can plan for costs in the tens of thousands if you hire a contractor. If you don't have those skills I strongly recommend that you hire an inspector first. If it is a fixer-upper, you are taking on enough cost to make the few hundred dollars for hiring an inspector inconsequential, and if it needs a lot of repair it is essential to know exactly what it needs before calling around for estimates, so I recommend you do so if this is the situation you are in.

With the benefit of hindsight I now believe that every renter in a rent-to-own deal should first hire an inspector to let them know what the home needs. It only cost us $800 to have the inspection at closing and had we done it up front it would have given us a lot more peace of mind knowing that we were going to pass rather than waiting on pins and needles to get the word back in time to meet our closing deadline. I was frugal and do not regret my decision, but really, the $800 would have been worth it.

Time to Learn some Skills

There was about six weeks of initial work that we had to do on the house before we could fully move in. Because we moved across town, this also allowed us to slowly move our things in as we made trips to the house to do general upgrades. Our biggest project was the basement. We spent weeks cleaning and converting it into a mother-in-law apartment. The upstairs of our rental alone was larger than the last two apartments we lived in combined. Because of this we saw an opportunity as we knew we could live with little space and stuff. We couldn't even fill the upstairs. It seemed empty to us after living in such a cramped space for so long. Rather than live on top of an empty basement, we worked to get some equity out of it.

We were regularly up until 2am working on that basement after work, along with long fourteen hour days on the weekends, in an effort to create a safe and cozy living space. It left us very tired with some sore backs, but it turned out to be one of the smartest things we did.

The more work we did, the more money we saved. Friends with skills helped. Youtube videos proved to be a valuable resource as we had to learn or remember old skills of patching drywall and painting. We learned how to install a laminate floor almost exclusively from Youtube videos. This was a key skill as two rooms had rotten carpet, and laminate flooring looks nice and is inexpensive and easy to install. I recall an inspector asking if the wood floors were new. I replied, "they are laminate and that is the best compliment I could receive as Allison and I put those in." He took note and I do not believe that hurt the assessed value.

It is difficult to assess the value of all of the work we did. It would certainly be in the thousands of dollars. Having a housemate renting our mother-inlaw over 20 months subtracted $17,000 from our expenses. So all of the work we put into our basement mother-in-law was easily worth the bags under the eyes and sore muscles.

After doing the work to our rental home, I was very happy that we did not choose to go the complete fixer-upper route. I consider myself pretty handy and willing to learn new skills, so a fixer-upper appealed to me. They are affordable, but buyer beware as the more of a fixer-upper you choose the more hard work you will have to do. If you can afford to pay others to do the work, you can probably afford to buy through conventional means. Contractor costs are not cheap, and if they are then you often get what you pay for. Costs run much higher for houses that have issues with roofs or water damage. Mold or infestation of any kind can be costly. Hidden costs can lurk everywhere behind the walls. Any number of problems that you inherit in a fixer-upper can cause other problems as well. It is important to know what you are getting in to if you are thinking about renting to own a home in poor condition.

We did have to use one contractor to get the home ready for anyone to live in because it had a clogged sewer pipe. Our next door neighbor has giant hedges that are bending the pipe down under their weight, creating a belly where debris collects as sludge and eventually clogs.

Anything going in the drain bubbled sewage up into the basement. A good plumber came out on a Saturday and cleared the pipe without any digging. A total cost of $750 and we could flush again. The cleanup that followed was the worst part of that mess. It took renting an expensive professional carpet cleaner for another$300 and many passes over three days before we were clean and sanitary again.

Our furnace did not work due to a blown capacitor, and the repairman and parts cost just over $250. These were both problems that I knew I could not fix with Youtube videos and tool rentals. I did do some research on easy troubleshooting and assessing issues. Capacitors can hold a strong electrical charge even after they are blown. Had I tried removing it myself and made a mistake, which is not unlikely, it could have been serious for my health. I did not put a price on my health when considering projects to get our home. If I thought either of us were going to be unsafe I called in a professional to do the job. I urge you to do the same. If you do not get your home due to contractor costs it probably was not in the cards anyway, as it might have been too much of a fixer-upper for your budget or too much of a distraction from your career. Live to go on another day and find a much better rent-to-own home to buy.

Used Stuff vs New Stuff

With the amount of work that our home needed and with how much money we knew we had to save, we had some difficult decisions to make in how to fix and replace the parts of the house and appliances that were broken. I learned a bunch of new skills to make repairs, but we had to buy some appliances as well.

If you have ever shopped for appliances you know they do not come cheap. For our mother-inlaw apartment we needed a refrigerator, microwave, dish washer, washer/dryer, range, lumber and painting supplies, an overall expense that quickly became five figures which was way out of our price range.

I checked Craigslist for used appliances and found a range for $50. I had to drive 90 minutes one way to meet the couple. They lived out in the Washington hills west of Centraila. There is nothing out there, not even a cell phone signal. It may have made some people too nervous to go out there and meet strangers with $50 in their pocket and no way to call for help, but I could not find a better deal anywhere, so I went for it. It turned out to be a sweet old couple who had a huge garage and lots of stuff stored in there. They had tons of great used stuff and offered to sell me a bunch of other things I needed just as cheap as long as I got it out of their garage for them. They helped us save a lot.

Craigslist is a great place to find quality used anything for cheap. Learning how to use Craigslist saved us a boatload of money. All I had to learn was how to sift through the junk. Learning that consisted of calling and emailing in response to tons of ads and then having conversations with the sellers. It only takes a few minutes to hear a shady deal shaping up. Genuine deals shined right through and arrangements were made quickly as it became clear the only agenda legit sellers have is to complete a fair deal. I have heard a few stories of people finding their rent-to-own dream homes listed on Craigslist. I didn't include that in Chapter Seven because I have no experience using Craigslist for finding a rent-toown, but it seems worth noting.

We also found a number of people willing to trade their quality used items for other items or skills they may need. Allison is a talented web developer and offered to make websites for people in exchange for stuff we needed, but in the end we only found one taker for a trade and we decided not to do it. You may have more trade opportunities than we did and next to getting something for free, a trade can save you the most money.

While Craigslist.org was a big money saver for us, the biggest was a Seattle business called "Second Use" that sells quality used building supplies. We found everything we needed at Second Use, and their prices are amazing. They sell everything salvageable from anywhere. They have everything from working 1920s appliances pulled out of old Seattle homes to industrial safes and filing systems salvaged from a Microsoft upgrade. I was like a kid in a candy store there and I still am every time I go.

Second Use also sells painting supplies including reusable paints from a company in Oregon called Metropaint. Metropaint gathers up paint from Oregon residents and then treats and repackages it and sells it at a fraction of the cost of new paint. It comes with a warranty, just like new paint, and coats in one pass. We know this from experience as we painted our entire house, inside and out, with Metropaint. Painting the outside was a big job and I enlisted some help from a friend of mine who is a professional painter. We painted with just regular Metropaint colors, nothing mixed, in tasteful and timeless shades. The "misty gray" color used on the outside coated the house in one pass using a standard roller on an extension poll. My painter friend continually raved about how thick and rich a coat the paint put on our house and continued to ask me the price as he could not believe how affordable it was. Neighbors still compliment us on the colors and the paint job itself.

There are some other great businesses in Seattle that sell salvaged used building supplies, but we had such a great experience at Second Use that we found ourselves back there over and over again. Check around your area for similar businesses. They are all over the place and can be a key to saving enough money to close on your home. Habitat for Humanity stores similarly offer great deals on quality used items, and Habitat for Humanity stores are located in more communities than salvage stores like Second Use. Habitat for Humanity stores are raising money for a great cause as well.

What this taught us is that used can be every bit as good and tasteful as new. Most importantly it saves a lot of money that we desperately needed to close the deal. You will likely need to save as much as possible as well. I can't make this point enough: if you sink a lot of money into upgrading your rental home and do not close the deal you will be wondering if those dollars spent on new furniture or appliances were worth it. Be frugal and do not be afraid of "used" supplies.

Moving in

Getting settled is an important part of a move. You want to feel at home and make your place nice so you are motivated to fight hard to close the deal. What you want to avoid is spending a lot of money on design. By design I mean furniture, appliances, and updates that might be due for upgrades, but are not necessary. There are a lot of people who have to have all new stuff, and you may be one of those people. Remember to avoid becoming your own enemy to closing the deal. Fixing and upgrading things that are not broken will set you back in closing on your home.

There are people who have to have matching appliances. I have met these folks. One appliance breaks and the others are all silver x brand so the new replacement has to be a silver x brand or they all will have to be replaced. There are also those who simply can't live with an outdated style. If your house has old false wood panel walls, like ours, it could be impossible for some people to accept. We are still ignoring ours because they are in good shape and not worth the cost of replacing.

If you fall into any of these camps or any others that value personal preference and wants over needs, be aware that you will potentially spend yourself out of closing on your lease option home. You will have to make a lot of difficult decisions. New appliances can wait until you close on your home. It's the same with new furniture or new walls or a bathroom remodel. If it is necessary work to make the home habitable and safe for you to live, then do it. If not, wait to do the upgrade. Good things come to those who wait anyway, and that good thing could be the paperwork that says you own the house. Reward yourself with new stuff. If you value that, use how much it bothers you as motivation to close the deal. Getting new stuff will never feel better than as a reward for your new house. If the house you are thinking about renting to own has quirky things that bother you enough that you can't live with them, then it might be best to look for a different rent-toown opportunity.

Try to make your move as inexpensive as possible as well. We were fortunate that we had six weeks of back and forth trips to slowly move most of our things in. The large items waited until actual moving day when we borrowed a friend's van. Everything fit into the van and all it cost us was some sore muscles and a $70 tank of gas. One great tip I have learned is to use liquor store boxes for moving. They aren't large boxes so they don't get overly heavy even when packed with books. They are designed to be sturdy enough to protect glass, come with dividers for your fragile items, and they're free for the asking at your local purveyor of wine and spirits. They also do not stink like many grocery store boxes do, and if you have used enough banana boxes then you know what I am talking about. If you do not mind your neighbors' first impression of you as a potential epic drinker you can save your back and a lot of money. Moving can be a big cost if you hire people and buy boxes.

Overall, try to make your move and set your house up without touching your savings or compromising how much you have budgeted to add to your savings during that quarter. That means you will likely have little to nothing to spend on home upgrades that are not completely necessary. If you need it in order to live there, then get it. If not, be very careful. Remember all of these things when you are scrambling to close because it can be really hard to close the deal. If you had to have a new couch and all the matching living room suite that goes with it and end up a few hundred dollars short at closing you could be sitting on your dreams. I just cannot stress this point enough.

Finding your lease option home is exciting. Enjoy it. Have a house warming party and make the space yours, but do it with a strategy to save money.

What you want to avoid is feeling too much like you actually purchased the home. It can cause you to believe that the most difficult part of the purchase is behind you, but trust me, it is not. At this point the hardest part will be building up a savings, improving and maintaining your credit, and closing the deal. Remember that you already know how our story ends, and we tried to close five times before it was over and almost did not get our home. It may not feel like it, but if you've come this far in your rent-to-own journey, you've actually come through the easiest part.

Chapter Checklist:
___Negotiate the terms of your lease option contract.

___Negotiate a 30 month lease option with an additional six month window to complete the deal if you are in the process of closing at the 30 month mark (a potential total of three years).

___Look the home over for signs anything is in need of repair.

___Ask the home owner what they know about the home especially anything in need of repair.

___Research public records associated with the property for more information.

___Learn what the FHA requirements are for a Federal-backed home loan.

___Decide whether or not to get an inspection.

___If a problem or need arises, research it to see if it is a potential do-it-yourself (DIY) project.

___Research which tools the job needs; the fewer and

more basic the tools the better the DIY potential.

___Ask family and friends with skills for their help.

___Look for "How To" videos on Youtube and watch as many as you can.

___Recognize if you need to call a repair man.

___Avoid getting in over your head. Be certain to get as comprehensive of a contract as possible. This takes more time and negotiation but protects all parties involved.

___Do not invest a lot in furniture and appliances (unless they are needed), rather focus on saving for your closing.

___Make your move as inexpensive as possible (ask for help).

___Do not trick yourself into believing that the journey is over. Once you are in a rent-to-own home your journey is just beginning.

> "We can't help everyone, but every-
> one can help someone."
>
> Ronald Reagan

ASKING FOR HELP

Writing a book about how to get your rent-toown home and not focusing on the need for help would be setting anyone interested in this option up for a very difficult, if not impossible journey. You are going to get a lot of help anyway and you are going to need it, so you might as well ask for it specifically when you do. I often wondered how many of the failed rent-to-own deals fell through because the buyers were too proud or afraid to ask someone for help. Not to imply that it is impossible, but I can't imagine how we would have been able to close without help. We got nearly half of our down payment from people helping us. With that help we saved a total of $50,000 even though we did not need quite that much in the end. When you add up all of the advice from realtors, lawyers, homeowners, family, friends, neighbors and even YouTube users who post free "how to" videos, that dollar amount increases significantly.

People are really nice. I know it doesn't always seem that way in traffic, but we are all pretty good people.

A lot of us know something really well, and we like to be the experts at it. We like to teach and share our skills with others. If you have a question about something in your home, ask someone for their help. People will often accept a trade if you have valuable skills to offer. Even if you do not, you can still offer to help out with a project that they may have. The worst thing that can happen is someone says no. That really is not that bad of an outcome, and when you know the worst outcome is a small two letter word, asking for help is not really scary at all. When the potential outcomes are "status quo" getting told "no because ___(insert excuse)___" or "getting your problem solved" those are not bad outcomes either way and the last outcome is solving your problem.

You can start asking for help right away with the seller, and ask them for an open-ended lease when negotiating the terms of your contract. Let them know that this will be a big help to you. Set a goal of no less than two years, and let them know that it is your intention to close within that window of time, but an open-ended lease helps give you the security of really investing your time and energy into their home. Two years is a very short window of time to save lots of money and rehab poor credit. It is about the minimum time frame to set yourself up for a successful rent-to-own. 30 months with a six month window to extend if you are already in the process of getting financed is probably the sweetest spot for both a serious seller and a motivated buyer.

147

Another benefit to an open-ended lease is that in most cases you have to be employed steadily at the same place for at least two years in order to be eligible for financing. Should you lose your job, keep in mind that an open-ended lease allows you the security of going out and getting another good job and staying employed for at least two years to get the deal done. It is also more time to save and get your credit score up, so even losing a job can be okay in a rent-to-own situation depending on how employable you are and the time frame you have to close the deal. Open-ended leases can be a problem as well. The problem with waiting too long is that bad things can happen along the way that can set you back. You have to find a nice balance of a window of time that allows you to save money and rehab your credit, but also is not so long that you get comfortable putting off attempting to close the deal.

Next is family. My Dad was a big help as we chose not to get an inspection up front, which in hindsight was not a good decision. We knew nothing about our major appliances, water heater and furnace, which are natural gas, so we were worried about them. After working for more than 30 years on just about everything related to natural gas my Dad is a pro. We have a gas line coming into the house and a gas furnace and water heater. Like I said, I don't know a thing about these appliances. They seem to work fine, but are they in need of repair or replacement? Are we going to end up sinking our savings into cleaning up a basement and getting a new water heater? In about ten minutes he was able to tell me just about everything about the furnace and water heater, roughly how old they are, and that they are high efficiency and in very good shape. With some regular maintenance (filters mostly) and attention we could rest easy regarding everything gas-related in the home. That was a great help and a lot of good time spent with my Dad.

A few friends referred us to one of the best realtors in Seattle, Sean Stolte, who at the time was with a local Berkshire Hathaway real estate office. They swore he helped them get their dream home. We called Sean up to let him know how highly regarded and recommended he was and to ask him if he would take a look at our situation to see if he would be willing to be our realtor as we approached our self-imposed closing deadline. He agreed to meet us, and it was pretty late on a workday; I believe it was after 6pm. Sean walked us through everything step by step. He researched what each house in a .25 mile radius of our home was selling for. He let us know we found a heck of a deal given how hot the Seattle market was at that time and we took a look at similar homes. Home after home in our neighborhood, some larger, but most smaller, were consistently selling for much more than the locked-in price on our lease option agreement, often$60,000 to $80,000 more. As the interview concluded Sean recommended we try to close the deal ourselves. He explained that we had come pretty far, were getting a heck of a deal, and that his services would not push us all that farther along and would cost at least $6,000. We took his advice, and it was some of the best that we received.

We inherited a pile of rubbish in the backyard big enough to hide a large SUV. It was infamous in the neighborhood, an eye sore that had been sitting there for years. We dressed up in some old clothes, took a beautiful Saturday, and started bagging it up. We quickly ran out of space in our rubbish bins and did not even put a dent in the pile. Neighbors remarked as they walked by how glad they were that someone was actually going to clean up the pile. As the day drew on and the bags piled up, neighbors came by offering to let us use their yard waste bins that would otherwise be empty that week. It was incredibly nice and thoughtful of them. We gladly took them up on it and we packed them full. Each neighbor who offered saved us $50 for pickup. Other neighbors offered to take smaller limbs out of the pile and chip them up with their wood chippers to add to their compost bins. This was a dirty job and any help was welcomed. It ended up costing us almost $400 to have the bags picked up. That is a pretty big chunk of change, but it would have cost us hundreds more if neighbors had not offered some help. In this case it was less our asking for help and more not being too proud to take help that was offered. They might have even been a bit motivated by having the pile gone and did not want us to give up as it literally took us all day to get rid of that ugly pile, and the summer days are long in Seattle.

One's motivation for helping you does not matter. The best relationships that you will build on your path to

150

your rent-to-own home are those based on solving problems for each side. Just accept their offer and the help if you can use it, and see if you can help solve a problem for them. In the weeks that followed we planted a berry patch in that spot. Now, rather than an ugly rotting pile of rubbish we enjoy fresh strawberries, raspberries, blackberries, blueberries and huckleberries. That spot now produces more berries than we can eat, and we leave the patch open to share the harvest with our neighbors.

Taking over the reins of home ownership can become very time consuming and costly. In most cases when you agree to a lease option you also agree to be responsible for the upkeep of the property. Things happen all the time and they can cost you money. I am at best an average handy man. I have some tools that I can use, I love to learn something new, and I like taking on a good project, so I was determined to become a do-it-your-selfer. It added up to big savings and we absolutely needed to save as much money as possible. Allison and I quickly identified the basement as a rental opportunity. It had a separate entrance, bathroom and bedroom. It had wall to wall carpeting, and while not a posh apartment, I had certainly lived in a lot worse. We needed to install a range, refrigerator and sink. This required I learn plumbing and electrical skills that I never had. I had only attempted one plumbing project before, and it went okay, but I knew it was amateurish work. I had never attempted to do any electrical work before, and I knew that could get expensive and even deadly.

I wanted to see all of the angles on home repair: safety, legality, permitting, etc., so I did an internet search and quickly found the answers to my questions. I found permit FAQs on the city's page that answered those questions. The Seattle fire department is an excellent resource for fire prevention information. It is a hard thing to put a price on. I called around to electricians, plumbers, and appliance stores. Many of them provided some helpful nuggets of information, but what I found was some of the most helpful people on Earth are YouTube users. There are people out there in the world who are really good at things and they like to share their talents and skills with you and for free on YouTube. I found step-by-step instructions for every household project you could imagine.

Not everyone who is willing to share on Youtube is an expert. I recommend watching a few how-to videos for each project you want to take on. You will get different perspectives and helpful tips by watching a few videos. You can also tell the good advice from the bad as you watch a lot of instructional videos. Some people do not know what they are talking about, and others are experts in their field but are terrible teachers. Find those who know how to give informative step-by-step instructions and who know what they are talking about. If I was new to a type of project, I needed the basic 101, entry level, dumbed-down lesson. If I had general knowledge and some experience on a particular project, I wanted lessons a bit more in-depth that took some liberties assuming I already had general knowledge. These were all found on Youtube and more than I actually needed on any given topic were usually there. I did almost all of the work on the basement mother-in-law myself, and I learned a ton along the way. Even with being willing to study and learn new skills and work well into the night on a regular basis I certainly could not have pulled it off without people's help on Youtube. All of the skills I learned came from someone else's expertise and their willingness to teach me for free.

We had a mother-in-law basement to rent with little additional investment other than time spent researching and learning and some elbow grease and tired backs. This was a key factor in us getting our home. With $600 per month rent coming in, an absolute steal in Seattle, we knocked our monthly rental payment down to $840 per month. This is also an absolute steal in Seattle. We created a situation in which we got a deal of a lifetime from a home owner who was about to lose his house to a big bank; we payed that forward by giving a young student-apprentice a nice affordable first apartment. We all helped each other because we all asked for help and were not too proud to accept the help of others. In hindsight $600 per month (no utilities or other costs) was too low of an amount to charge for the apartment. It barely covered month to month expenses associated with having a renter. Our current housemate splits the mortgage with us at $750 per month (and also pays no utilities or other costs). This makes it a better financial arrangement to have a housemate, and still gives everyone a great deal in an expensive city like Seattle.

What this experience taught us was that helping people brings more help from people. Allison explains it with the folk tale "Stone Soup". If you are not familiar with "Stone Soup," it is set in a poor community struggling with famine. One family decides to share the only thing they have left with their entire neighborhood, a pot of water. That family prepares a fire out in front of their home. They place a large pot filled with water on the fire to simmer, and then with nothing else to offer they add a few clean stones and rocks. Then they offer to share their stone soup with their hungry neighbors. Curious neighbors see or happen upon the simmering soup. They too are very poor and hungry. They too have little to nothing to eat, let alone much to offer others, but one by one the neighbors are curious to see what the family has cooking. As they see the pot of simmering rocks they also see a vision for a meal. Moved to act, the townspeople gather whatever edible scraps they happen to have left in their homes and one by one they add them to the pot of boiling rocks. One family adds carrots, another an onion, another some greens, another brings beans, and this continues. Before long the entire community is enjoying an unthinkable feast.

This classic tale helps to illustrate a couple of key components you will need to know in order to close the deal on your home: take action even when it seems silly, do not be afraid to ask for help or to accept help from others, and try to solve a problem for those that help as well. Beyond that what we found was, just like the "Stone Soup" tale, taking action brings about more action and asking for help actually brings more help. What happened in our home purchase was almost as magical as the classic folk story.

It is highly unlikely that we could have gotten our home without help. A lot could have happened in that time, so to think that it would have worked out just as we had planned and budgeted is not likely. We moved when we initially planned and it really showed our friends and family that we were serious serious about our goals and were ready to own a home. I do believe it was that constant focus on our goal of closing the deal at eighteen months and really going for it at that point that helped us build the momentum that resulted in so many people who were willing to do what they could to help us. That old cliché is right: "Just ask. The worst that will happen is someone will say no." What is most telling about asking for help is that while the possibility of someone saying no is the scariest before you ask, now that we own our home I can't remember a single no outside of the mortgage brokers we initially met with. I recall those no's because I used them as motivation to get through the most difficult times. Mostly, I only remember the yes's because they believed in us and without them I doubt we would be living in our home today. So overcome the fear of being told "no" by focusing on the excitement and anticipation of working with and solving a problem for those who say yes.

I hope that you remember this chapter when you find yourself stuck during your rent-to-own journey. If you do look for help and ask for it I believe you will be more likely to succeed in getting your home. The more obstacles you conquer along the way, the more confidence in yourself you will have moving forward. When people see confidence in you, you will inspire them to have confidence in you as well.

Chapter Checklist:

___Accept that you will need help.

___Remember the best mutually beneficial relationships happen when you can solve a problem for the person helping you solve your problem.

___Take action: doing so will help you overcome any fear of asking for help because taking action makes more action happen.

___Help takes a lot of different forms, so take what you can get— advice, discounts, trades, phone calls, etc.

___Do not forget to say thank you to those who help you.

___Anytime you feel like giving up, remember your goal and remember that if it feels too hard you probably just need to ask for some help.

___Search Youtube how-to and lesson videos on nearly every topic imaginable.

"I have tried raising money by asking for it, and by not asking for it. I always got more by asking for it."

Millard Fuller

RAISING MONEY

I was like most people, not much better at raising money than I was at saving money, but if you are in a situation like we were, you will have to learn how to do it.

There are a lot of ways to raise money for your home purchase. We will examine a few of the ways that we explored as we approached our closing date. Those are personal assets, friends and family, and crowd funding websites.

These three fundraising sources are pretty easy to set up and put in motion, but all require a lot of hard work to get value back. What is more of a barrier to raising money than the hard work involved is that for many people, these all seem incredibly uncomfortable and because of that, many will let this opportunity to raise money for their home pass them by. If you find a home that is a great investment for you and your family and money is the only barrier, please raise money. Just do it. There is no reason to sit in your comfort zone if it leads you to miss out on your family's happiness. Remember that it is always better to be uncomfortable than unhappy. I imagine that being comfortable in an unhappy life is a pretty miserable existence. To each their own, I have always believed that, but getting comfortable with being unhappy means you are cashing in any hope for a happy life. Be very careful with that if getting your rent-to-own home is part of your vision for a happy life. I am not comfortable when I am unhappy, so I find myself jumping out of my comfort zone and pushing life toward a happier place a lot. Stepping out of your comfort zone will open up doors for you and help you achieve your difficult goals all throughout life, so use your rent-to-own purchase to get good at it.

Why is asking for money so uncomfortable?

This answer will be different for everyone. Consider if it is uncomfortable for you, and if it is, why? Maybe you do not like being asked for money, and because the reaction you feel when asked is an uncomfortable one, you assume that the same burden that you feel is shared by all. That is false. Not everyone is totally annoyed by those who ask for money. In fact, there are people who have a lot of money, who are always looking for people to help and invest in. They invest in people for a living. Think about that for a minute. While some people are annoyed that anyone would have the guts to even approach them to ask for money, others are actually waiting for opportunities to give money to people to help them with their investments. In the end they know they will invest in the right people and those people will solve a problem and add enough value to the world to pay them back at a profit.

You may be thinking, "I do not know any investors, and if I do they do not invest in rent-toown homes, so how is my rent-to-own home related to an investor?" The bank is making an investment in you, your home and your ability to pay for it. They most certainly are investors. You are going to ask them for a lot of money and if they loan it to you, they will make a profit on your ability to pay it back through the interest attached to the loan. Investing is already an integral part of the home buying process and in a lot of ways you as the home buyer are the investment. Because the deal we negotiated with our seller was such a spectacular investment, the bank was far more motivated to fund our loan.

In our case we have parents who couldn't help us out with a great deal of money, but they were surprisingly willing to offer up what they could. I recall feeling uncomfortable with every single person we asked to help us with money, but I do not recall a single person reacting in a negative or uncomfortable way. I do not even recall who said no. The only person who was uncomfortable with me asking for money was me. Had I not asked I would have assumed that I did them all a favor by not putting them in that uncomfortable position. In reality they all wanted to help out any way they could. I had to ask to know that. You should remember that and be sure to ask if you need help raising money.

Personal Assets

Part of raising money is finding money you have already earned at some point in life. You may be well aware of all personal assets that you have in your name, but maybe not. A number of jobs that I have left over the years offered 401Ks as a supplemental retirement benefit. I utilized my 401K for part of our down payment to close our rent-to-own home. I encourage you to weigh the pros and cons of dipping into your 401K and pension investment benefits. Depending on the state of your 401K, compounding interest could be reason enough to leave that 401K alone until retirement.

In addition to your current 401K, look for old 401ks from previous jobs. You might be sitting on enough money for your down payment just from an old 401K or two. They are out there and if you put in some years of service at an old job you might have accumulated a few thousand dollars that is just sitting there. Contact your old jobs and talk to human resources to see what you have to do to find out.

If you have a current 401K, you might be able to withdrawal a portion or take a loan out on it if this is your first home purchase. As I mentioned this is something I did to help raise money. In my case I had to take a loan out on my 401K as they did not allow any withdrawals. It will not show up on your credit report. If it would show up on your credit report you should not do this as it could prevent you from getting financing from the bank.

Taking out loans on our 401Ks is a risk that we both decided to take, but not until we were right up to the gun on closing on our home. We did this because setting money aside for retirement is a lot like a savings account, meaning the same rules apply, and through this home purchase we really did come to appreciate how important a growing saving is. We wanted to keep our 401Ks untouched until it became apparent that closing on our home would actually be a better long-term investment than the 401K itself. Once we reached that point we both decided to take out the loan to help close the deal. I still think refusing to touch your 401K is best until you know you are going to close and your money from your 401K is necessary to make that happen. In other words, leave your retirement savings accounts alone unless you absolutely need them to close the deal on your home. Even then your home has to be a good enough investment to justify reaching into your 401K. In our case it was obviously so, given that my 401K benefit, after three years of employment, was sitting at just $9,000 when I was 36 years old and our home was already carrying roughly$100,000 worth of equity. Your situation might not be so obvious. Allison's 401K was at nearly $40,000 and with compound interest we actually decided to not use any of her retirement savings to buy our home. If you have to walk away leaving a bunch of money in a house, do not leave your retirement in it as well. It could be devastating for you down the line in life. Every decision has to be a calculated risk. Do not take your retirement lightly.

I simply cannot stress to you how important it is to respect your 401K as a good long-term personal investment. Weigh your options thoroughly as you decide whether or not to use your it for your home purchase. For me, in my mid-thirties with only three years invested in my 401K, it was clear that compounding interest was not going to help me as much as the red-hot Seattle real estate market potentially could. I would have been working well into my 70s or 80s to see the type of cost benefit that would have given me pause regarding my 401K. Rather, our home was holding all of that equity at that time. It was easy to see that was a far better investment than the $9,000 I had in my 401K. That is a good example of making a cost benefit analysis. The cost of taking out a loan on my 401K was worth the benefit we gained in getting our home. The cost of cashing out any portion of Allison's was not as obvious. The long-term benefit of her 401K investment may have been as good as the long-term benefit of the equity on our home, so the cost of pulling money out of her larger 401K in her early 30s may not have been worth the benefit of getting our home. It just was not clear as compound interest can trigger significant gains for her 401K later in life. Because of taking some time to do these cost benefit analyses I was prepared to invest all $9000 into our home. My 401K provider only allowed a loan up to 50% for a first time home purchase. I took all I could and added it to our growing savings.

"Calculated risks." I could have tattooed those two words on my body somewhere as we weighed every decision this way. You should as well.

One factor we talked about as a part of our discussion regarding our 401Ks was a very timely Frontline documentary called "The Retirement Gamble" that aired April 23, 2013 on PBS. April of 2013 saw us exactly one year into our rent-to-own journey. Just as we were weighing our options to make our plan so we could prepare for our closing target date that Frontline aired. Part of the plan was to immediately start inquiring with our employers as to if we could access our 401Ks, how we access our 401Ks, and if we should at all, so the documentary was influential in our decision to access our retirement benefits. You should watch "The Retirement Gamble", but to briefly summarize, some companies that manage 401Ks are transferring your compounding interest to themselves by way of the fees. They collect those seemingly small fees early on in your employment, but over time the fees add up. What is supposed to happen is that money is supposed to be adding up in your retirement account to become the compounding interest that eventually allows you to retire later in life. In other words the compound interest associated with those fees becomes serious money for those companies who are taking small fees from many, many hard workers. Money that is supposed to make it a decent supplemental retirement for the beneficiary accumulates into a large pool of money that pays off as compounding interest for the company.

Do not let this reference to the Frontline documentary scare you. It is not intended to influence you into taking money from your 401K plan. I am including it to give some perspective as to how complex this kind of investing is. At the time it aired I was really struggling with whether or not it was a good decision to take a loan out of my 401K to help with the down payment on our home. "The Retirement Gamble" helped me see that even seemingly safe long-term investments can suffer unforeseen costs, and were even as much of a gamble as our rent-to-own home.

The 401K plan at both of our employers were reputable. Allison's especially was quite good, and we often remarked how her plan was one of the better benefits that any adjunct professor could hope for. But I do not know enough about how the fee system worked to be completely confident that I was not losing out on compound interest. We explored our financial decisions from as many angles as we could. Perhaps it was all in the timing of when we happened to see "The Retirement Gamble," but it did influence my decision to withdrawal half of my 401K. However, I did withdraw that money in the form of a loan that I am paying back to myself. By paying it back I am going to get most of the compound interest back in the end. Taking money out of your 401K is risky. It should not be done lightly. I encourage you to research your 401K for yourself. In the end, out of nearly $50,000 in combined benefits we only withdrew $4,500 from my 401K in the form of a loan. In this instance I want you to see that we took a very calculated risk. We ended up with both our home and our 401Ks.

We had other smaller personal assets that together raised a decent chunk of our down payment money. You could probably do the same. Start having yard sales, sell your toys, sell an extra vehicle if you have one. If you like having a pickup truck just in case you have to haul something, but do not use it as your regular vehicle, sell it. It is probably bad on gas anyway, which also cuts into your savings. If you have a camper for the occasional trip up to the mountains, sell it and get a tent. We actually had a nice older camper van that we loved. The Pacific Northwest has some of the best outdoor recreation in the U.S., and we have two dogs. A camper van made going camping with dogs much more fun and easy than in a tent, but it only got used a few times a year so it had to go. Our hatchback with a tent is much better on gas and we still make a lot of great memories which is really what a camping trip is all about.

You might be surprised at just how much money you are sitting on right now as you read this. See for yourself and start to build your savings. Toys are expensive and we often end up giving them away anyway. Your home can help you realize part of your American dream. It can allow you to pass wealth down through your family for generations. Prioritize those goals and sell, sell, sell your stuff if you have to. Sell off anything that is not going to pass generational wealth down through your family. That means letting go of sentimental attachment. Just because something associated with a family member has some value to you personally does not mean that any other person, family included, will ever place any value on that item at all. Sentimental value is worthless in terms of providing for your family. Do not let it hold you back from making a great investment.

Get creative with how you raise money. Once we were renting to own the home we were in, all of the extra space became a kind of personal asset. We lived in tiny mother-in-law cottages before finding our home. Our new rental house seemed huge. As I mentioned before we decided that we would put a mother-in-law style apartment in our basement and get a housemate. It was an affordable rental option for a bunch or our friends, but also a way for us to immediately start to get value out of our new personal asset.

Friends and Family

After we made our plan to raise or save at least enough for a 20% down payment (over $40,000) we knew we had to make asking family a part of that plan. It was not necessary to ask them right away. We did not even know exactly how much we would need to ask for yet, and we may not have needed any help at all. It was just too early to tell.

As the months passed and our savings grew we

thought that we were not going to have to ask anyone in our families for help. I recall mentioning that it might not come down to us needing any financial help, but my Dad offered to help us out anyway. I let him know that I appreciated the offer but I was still relieved to have saved enough not to have to depend on his help.

When we first tried to close the deal I was sent out of town for work. My improving credit was still too low for an FHA loan anyway, so working with the bank Allison decided to try to get financed in just her name. I was fine with this as my out of town assignment was involved and took a great deal of my time and attention. She needed me to be ready to respond to needs with quick turn-around and I was not in a position to accommodate. Rather than wait out my stay, which dragged on twice as long as expected, financing Allison alone seemed like the best option.

What we learned was that on Allison's salary alone we would need a much larger down payment than the original 20% figure we were focused on. In fact, the bank was now asking for a $45,000 down payment. We had to either try to come up with an extra $6,000, which seemed impossible, or wait until after the holidays and try again in January or February which was months later. At this point we had to tell our families what was going on, and we felt like we finally had to ask them for financial help.

Allison's Dad had already sent her his contribution. As I have mentioned throughout the book we made a plan up front and worked hard to stick to it. Part of that plan was understanding that any large contributions of financial help from family would have to happen at least 60 days in advance of attempting to close in order to escape penalties for receiving a gift. Keep this 60 day window in mind as you make your plan, and check to make sure that the rules are not different where you live. Allison talked to her Dad, letting him know that we might need help but could not wait until the last minute due to the various rules associated with financial contributions. He helped in a big way by sending us $20,000, far more than we ever expected. We were floored by his willingness to help us close the deal. When he sent Allison that money we planned on giving it right back as we were certain we would not need it, given how much our savings was growing by the month. Unfortunately we did need it, and then some, due to the bank continuing to require a much higher payment with each closing attempt.

Allison and I had saved $19,000 on our own, for $1,000 per month average savings over the course of our rent-to-own contract which we were really proud to accomplish. Her Dad's $20,000 contribution took us to $39,000, just under our 20% goal, but the bank was telling Allison they needed $45,000. I had a timely paycheck I was willing to throw completely in and live off of tap water and peanut butter sandwiches, but that still left us nearly $5,000 short. I recalled my Dad's offer to help us, so I called him on a cold gray day in October and had to ask for money. He was happy to help us just like Allison's Dad. That did not make it easy to ask, but it was necessary so I did. He also over delivered, wiring $6000 to my bank account. With my paychecks and his contribution we were able to meet the bank's seemingly crazy demands. This was the moment we had worked so hard for, we overcame a huge financial hurdle right at the last minute, and we were confident because we did it right at the eighteen month mark, just as we planned when we started our purchase.

As we waited day after day for the news that our loan was funded, time dragged on. Even with seemingly impossible obstacles we somehow made it this far, and it was right on our target timeline. I got the call from Allison while I was watching a short winter day disappear through a window at work. We were denied by the final underwriter. The bank was now asking for a minimum of 40% which was well over $50,000 if they were going to fund Allison alone. We were devastated. With my out of town assignment dragging on and on and two major holidays looming, we were going to have to wait until the New Year and it could not be Allison alone. Even with savings from the first quarter of 2014 there was no way we could make the 40% any time soon. We eventually closed five months later, and getting there also required a lot of help, but thankfully not as much money.

It was not easy asking family for help. After the

dust settled and we closed the deal on our home, Allison's Dad explained to us that he received a lot of help to get his first home. He said that given his personal experience buying a home in the high interest rate era of the 1980s he didn't think it was possible without help. He was ready and willing to help all along. He was willing to pay forward help that we didn't know he received. Please do not be afraid to raise money as there could be people who are ready and waiting to help you.

Crowd funding

If after reading our story of asking our families for help you find yourself still too uncomfortable to ask family and friends directly, you should consider doing it through a crowd funding campaign. Crowd funding is still a relatively new phenomena, and is still evolving, but people have run some amazing fundraising campaigns for things a lot smaller than a house. A recent example that received a lot of attention is the Kickstarter campaign to raise money for a potato salad. If you have not heard, an Ohio man started a campaign to raise $10 so he could go buy ingredients to make a potato salad. He ended up raising over $50,000.

While not all campaigns are successful, they are all a ton of work. Crowd funding campaigns take good planning from the time you start preparing, months in advance, to seeing it through to the end.

Each crowd funding website offers great tips to help you achieve success and get through all of the layers of work that you have to do to. They make their money from taking fees from what you raise so it is in their best interest to set you up for success. If you try the crowd funding approach to a campaign, study as many of their best practice tips as you can and take their advice.

Not all crowd funding websites allow funding for the same things. We had a plan to crowd fund to raise money for our house but when we researched this option few crowd funding sites allowed raising money to invest which meant we were left out. In hindsight I wish we would have gotten more creative with our crowd funding ideas. For instance, we found that the many successful campaigns state their larger goal or objective, "to buy our first home", but raise money for a very specific small goal, "help us raise $10,000 to create an affordable basement apartment for a place for our friend to live." We could have tried something like that, but it was a ton of work and with the restrictions we decided against preparing a campaign only to be told we could not keep the money.

Since that time I have found some crowd funding sites that do allow raising funds for anything. Because we did not use one of these websites I can't give you any advice as to which one to choose and why. Because there are so many new start-ups getting into this space and I don't have a crystal ball, I am not going to try to guess which crowd funding website will be best for you to raise money for a home purchase on. Plan on looking at a few of them until you find the one that fits you best.

Crowd funding is a great option for you to raise money. Get creative with it. I truly wish we would have tried this option just to see what was possible. I like crowd funding so much because it is a microcosm of the American dream. Alone one might see me as a dreamer, but crowd funding changes that. If you have an idea, project, product or business that helps people solve a problem or that provides them with something they want, lots of people will happily chip in to help your dream come true. It is fun just to browse the campaigns and follow them to actually see people's dreams coming true with the help of hundreds (or thousands) of anonymous supporters.

If you decide to go the crowd funding route I recommend picking a few new campaigns that start around the same time and following them all the way through. See if any of them are successful and then compare those that are with those that are not. Cross reference what you observe with how they all interpret the best practice advice offered by the crowd funding website you choose. You will start to get a good picture of how to approach a campaign, and hopefully you get some creative ideas for a compelling ask.

We took the same strategy to raising money from outside sources, family and friends and personal assets, which was to save as much as we could by ourselves first then turn to raising money. We waited to ask for financial help until we were certain we knew we could close the deal, until we knew exactly how much to ask for, and until we could tell people why we were asking for that amount. As an example, if we were ready to close but thought we might be $3500 short, we would have a specific amount we needed and a compelling and timely ask. That is a much better way to raise money than just saying, "we need to raise $30,000 for a down payment on our home". By doing it the way we did, people could see that we could identify a great investment and that we could save and get all the way to the finish line to close the deal. They could come in and directly help us get there. We gave them space to come in and save the day and they did not disappoint.

Chapter Checklist:
Personal Assets:

___Forget sentimental attachment.

___Sell extra cars, trucks, campers, tools and other personal items that you do not use or need (even spare parts have value).

___Have a yard sale, use Craigslist and eBay.

___Research your 401K.

___Weigh this option carefully. Find out if they allow a loan or a withdrawal for a first home purchase to see how much you can raise this way should you need it.

___Offer to report rent payments to a credit agency through a company that processes automatic payments and reports to Rentbureau (see Chapter 4) to help your renter show that they make their payments on time.

Friends and Family:

___Talk with your family and friends about your plan to buy your home early and keep them informed of your progress.

___Have a clear plan and keep it up to date and ready to share.

___Wait until you know you need money and until you know an amount that will get you to closing.

___Be mindful of the rules limiting financial gifts for home purchases and plan accordingly.

Crowd funding:

___Find a few sites and read and study their best practice guides.

___Review the rules to make sure that you can raise money for something associated with your home purchase.

___Pick out a few campaigns on each site and follow them at least weekly to see which campaigns are successful.

___Identify how the successful campaigns use the best practice advice on the site.

___Review the campaigns that fail to meet their goals and learn from what those campaigns did that caused them to come up short.

___Wait to crowd fund until you have a specific amount, a specific goal, and a compelling ask.

___Be mindful that it takes some time to get access to the money you raise, so do not wait too long. Waiting for your crowd funding money will hold up your home purchase.

"The opposite of courage is not cowardice, it is conformity. Even a dead fish can go with the flow."

Jim Hightower

FOR SELLERS

If you are a homeowner or a landlord and reading this, you may be considering a lease with an option to sell as a way to rent and sell your home. There are advantages to this approach, even though lease options are far from common. Renting a property is always a risk. We became almost meta-landlords the day we moved into our rental home, and within the first year we learned a hard lesson about residential rentals which I will explain later in the chapter. We were working towards buying our home through the lease option provided by our seller and took on a housemate to live in the basement mother-in-law space that we created. This gave us the unique experience of both renting from a landlord and renting to a tenant at the same time. This added up to valuable experience for us that I will share here.

The pros and cons on both sides of the rent-to-own coin became very clear to us, and while offering a lease with an option to buy your property is not for everyone, there are reasons that everyone should be informed as to what the benefits and drawbacks of a lease option are. First I will examine the general thinking on the benefits of selling via rent-to-own. Then we will dive into our situation a bit deeper to look at the possibility to save homes from foreclosure. Then we will look at renting to own as an investment opportunity. After reading this chapter I hope you will have a more clear picture as to how you can set yourself up for success no matter what situation you are in or what you decide to do with your property.

General Rent-to-Own Advantages

In general there are some key advantages to becoming a lease option seller rather than simply renting your home. The first advantage is the length of the lease. In our case the homeowner gave us an open ended lease. If you find buyers you are confident in, I recommend offering them plenty of time to complete the deal. It also gives you a stable monthly rental income for far beyond the traditional one year lease.

There is also the cost savings in maintenance and repair. In a lease option agreement it is typical for the renter/buyer to be responsible for all maintenance and repairs to your property. In our case we began cleaning up the home, which had years of neglect from past renters who apparently did not feel invested in the property. We cleaned up the notorious rubbish pile in our alley. We fixed the outside sewage line, and this was not cheap but 100% necessary as sewage would flood the basement every time we ran any water down the drain. We had to paint the entire inside of the house, every wall. There was electrical work that needed repair, and the original hardwood floors in the living room were so bad that our sneakers would wear the finish off of them from simply walking from the front door to the kitchen. They needed to be refinished or risked being completely ruined. We decided to cover them with carpet to prevent any further damage from being done to them until we could afford to refinish them. We trimmed and landscaped the property; this took many weekends of work as the property was taken over by vegetation. I also cleaned moss off of the roof and I kept the gutters clean every fall.

Our landlord paid for none of this. I am not even certain if he knew the total extent of the work that his home needed and the care we were providing. We spent thousands of dollars on repairs and countless hours of work. When you rent to a motivated buyer who loves your home and wants to be there longterm, you will see a lot more attention and effort put into maintaining your property. In most rent-toowns that renter liability is memorialized in the contract you sign. If the deal should fall through for some reason, then you are far more likely to find your home better than when you rented it. Every situation is different but in general you will have a better experience with rent-to-own buyers than standard renters.

That being said, don't hide issues from the renters. If there is something that you know about you should be up front about all of it. Your honesty will inspire enough trust in the renter for them to take on those projects. They can make a plan to pay for and fix issues if they know about them. They will be less likely to have a big project, like a busted sewer pipe, cause them to walk away from the deal. It could come down to a simple cost-benefit analysis for them. Owning the home they truly want cancels out the sewer pipe expense if they are confident that you are helping them get the home.

If the inspector they hire discovers a lot of problems that you failed to disclose, they will have little faith in dealing with you. Create a contract that clearly solves a problem for both sides. Your problem may be finding a buyer at the price you desire, and their problem is likely to be that they have too little in their savings account or poor credit. If you are up front, they can perform the cost benefit and make a plan to fix the issues, absorb that cost, and still save enough to buy your home. Not disclosing expensive problems does not solve their savings problem. Rather, it makes your problems much worse and you make your odds of closing the deal much worse as well.

A lease with an option to sell your home gets you a non-refundable down payment called "option money" where a landlord typically gets a security deposit which can be partly refundable. In a lease option deal you get part of the down payment up front, usually 3% of the assessed value of the home. This gives you the security of knowing that the buyer can and has saved money. They are serious enough to put their money on the line and you get some financial benefit up front. In our case the seller received roughly 3% ($7,000) option money up front. This was the first big step to helping him solve the problem of saving his home from foreclosure.

Getting locked into a selling price is a bit of a gamble. Just like all gambling this can pay off or be a financial burden. If you are locked into a price to sell and the value of the property drops, you may have made a great decision to protect some of the equity in your home. If the converse happens, then you have to sell for less than you would make putting your home on the open market. Losing equity on value is not as bad as it sounds. As a seller you can make up for that in your monthly rental equity. No matter where you live, pay attention to what is happening with the real estate market to minimize the risks you are taking. A little information can go a long way to protecting your assets.

Beyond knowing your market, negotiate a price that limits your risk but still offers some potential reward to the buyer. They too are making a gamble. Our seller could have made nearly $150,000 more dollars by waiting and putting his home on the open market in the summer of 2014, but this point was moot because he was days away from losing the home to foreclosure back in early 2012. At that time he needed us as much as we needed him. He, like all of us, also had no way of knowing what was going to happen with the housing market from early 2012 until mid 2014. He was honest and held up his end of the bargain, and that honesty really paid off. Rather than give his home back to the bank, he saved it. He also did not have to find the $10,000 he needed to get his home back into rental shape. He also got a very helpful option money payment of$7,000 up front the day we signed the initial contract. On top of all of that, we paid him over $40,000 in rental equity along the way. After selling the home for $213,000, $40,000 in rent, $7,000 in option money, and the savings on repairs and maintenance he ended up getting approximately$270,000 out of a home he was going to lose along with the $209,000 that he still owed. In other words, by taking action and selling to us via rent-to-own he experienced a $480,000 difference in outcomes, pretty amazing, and the reason why Nathaniel Williams is one of the unsung heroes of the housing market crash, and of our story.

What our deal does not reflect is a rental premium. In some rent-to-own deals the renter will pay you an amount in premium rent with an amount greater than the mortgage payment. This is put into a savings account to be used to close the deal. That rental premium gives you piece of mind that the renter is saving to close on time. If you set something like this up you should do so through an escrow company to ensure payment goes to your mortgage holder and the agreed upon savings account. You can also set up a direct payment to your mortgage holder in which your renter sends the check directly to the bank. This is an advantage because it gives the renter the piece of mind they need to make a deal to buy a home if it is dangerously close to being foreclosed upon. If you are willing to give a renter the piece of mind that they are dealing with a honest and trustworthy person, then no matter how bad your situation seems, you will find a great buyer for your home.

Saving Your Home from Foreclosure

There should be a good picture developing as to how our seller was able to save his home from foreclosure through a rent-to-own sale. This is still a viable option for a lot of homeowners in his situation, so I want to go a bit deeper on the topic.

As the housing crisis begins to ease in some places, others are still mired in the same crisis they were in back in 2007. If you are in a state that is still in the housing crisis and you are a homeowner in danger of having your home foreclosed upon, then you should consider renting your home with a lease option to buy. If just a small percentage of the hundreds of thousands of homeowners who will lose their homes to foreclosure are able to follow the path of our seller, then we can save hundreds if not thousands of homes from the same fate. If any percentage of those homes saved go to first time homebuyers locked out of receiving credit by a wary banking system, then we are in a "save two birds with one worm" scenario in which two major problems with the housing market are addressed together through one rent-to-own purchase.

The only reason we were able to buy our first home in the red-hot Seattle real estate market is because our seller refused to give his home back to the bank. He weighed his options, got creative, and made a plan. You may recall from Chapter Six that he utilized an ad for his home on Zillow.com to sneak his phone number into the ad along with a message in quotes: "rent-to-own". Because he took action and was willing to sell rather than give up, he gave us the deal of a lifetime and we were able to finally buy our first home in the city we love not long after being turned away from mortgage brokers for much lesser homes.

If you are a victim of the housing crisis please do not give up. Start thinking of yourself as a hero rather than a victim and turn your situation around. We lived this first hand. We know that it can work. We knew we could afford a home, but we could not have done it without the seller. Working together we can simultaneously save homes from foreclosure and get young professionals or first time buyers with improving credit an opportunity the banks otherwise deny them.

I did meet other home owners who were resigned to lose their homes and wait the seven years or so until they were able to get back into the real estate market, and others who intended to stay away forever. Why give up? If it seems acceptable because there are a lot of other people in the same situation as you, think again. Misery loves company, but that is not the kind of company you should ever want to keep. Get proactive and take action to save your home. If it seems too risky to move out and become a renter while renting your home, think about the risk of having it get repossessed. If you are in danger of losing your home then you have nothing to lose in renting it to own, so go for it. Take action and become someone's hero. You might be surprised at how it pays off in the end.

It may be more work now to find a lease option buyer and move out into a rental unit, but it will allow you to quickly get back on your feet. The value of putting a little time into finding an alternative to losing your home could end up paying off for you in a big way; remember the $480,000 difference for our seller. Our seller ended up making money on the deal after all. It may not be what he envisioned when he he purchased the home as an investment opportunity, but making money is making money. It must be especially sweet when just two years earlier he was days away from losing the home for nothing. Given the potential to go from someone facing embarrassing financial ruin to being able to become an investor in a hot market is the difference between being a "dead fish" going with the flow or being a hero.

A good rent-to-own buyer will ask a lot of questions about your situation. Be honest with them. If you are dangerously close to losing the home, talk to them about your challenges. You want to rent to a potential buyer with thick enough skin to work overcome the problem. If you owe $10,000 show them the documentation. Let them know what is going on so they know that their option money is going directly to pay that amount off. If they love your home and are serious buyers, this will make them more likely to move in quickly to help you solve your problem with their option payment.

In order to make this happen, you should set up a deal with an escrow company or a note-servicing company in which the seller pays the escrow fees, the option money payment, and then the rental payments and savings that follow. For a fee that escrow company will ensure that their down payment goes to the money owed on the mortgage. This will give the renter the peace of mind to know that their investment is safe and that the money helped you and them.

Create as many win-win scenarios as you can for you and the renter. This will set you both up on a path of mutual benefit. It will also help you build a positive relationship with the person living in your home. If they trust that you are both working together, they will work hard to make sure that you are safe from foreclosure and you can, in turn help them stay on track to buy your home. Saving your home from a big bank repossession will be easier with someone in your corner, and in your house. First time home buyers in a difficult market will find their path to home ownership much smoother if they are working with the seller to close the deal.

If the servicing fees throw you, you can also set

up a payment directly to the mortgage holder. This could get tricky depending on how far down the road toward foreclosure you are. We did not need either of these options as our seller gave us such a sweet deal that we gave him almost total trust with our investment. That helped both parties keep from putting up barriers of distrust as the closing date approached. We took him at his word. He took us at our word. In the end he was an honest man who kept his promise and we were top notch renters who stayed out of his way and took great care of his property. Working together we did this and I am confident that you can as well.

Rent-to-Own As An Investment

Can renting to own your property or properties be a good investment for you? Yes it can, but just like rent-to-own buyers, you should be very cautious of who you deal with when it comes to investing this way. I ran into a lot of companies while researching for this book that offer to connect renters who want to buy a rent-to-own home with home owners who want to rent with an option to sell. Most of these companies have popped up since we found our home so I was curious to learn more about them.

One website in particular pitched their service by saying that you will save money on taxes should you choose to reinvest money you make on your real estate sale into another real estate purchase. While it is true that reinvesting money made on real estate into another real estate transaction is tax free, it does not mean that you will want to reinvest in real estate 2 or 3 years down the road when your home actually sells. That is how they justify their up front fee which in some setups would have been your option money. There are a couple of problems with this arrangement. First it assumes that you will gain equity on the property. This is not ever a guarantee. Second, it could be years down the road when your home actually sells and your plans may change, so you may end up paying a $10,000 fee and the taxes as well. I do not want to scare you into thinking that every listing service is taking advantage of people with poor credit or uninformed homeowners looking to invest. Just be prepared to ask them a lot of tough questions before you commit to any of these.

They will offer to set you up with other rent-to-own homes where you can use the money you make on the sale of the home you just sold through them to re-invest in the homes within their listing service. In other words, you sell your home via a lease option and then take the money you made on the deal (if you make money on the deal) to buy other homes from them and immediately rent-to-own those homes on their website. Each time this happens they get a fee which like before is likely to be what you would have gotten in option money.

Here is an example of how it would work. You, the seller, sell your home for $150,000. If you reinvest this money in real estate you get it tax free. Because of this the rent-to-own company can set you up with one or more homes depending on your willingness to invest and, in theory, you can immediately get some rent-to-own buyers into your new home(s). At the end of those lease option agreements, if the buyer is able to get financed you sell those homes as well and you gain more equity and continue to reinvest in even more homes that they offer. Again, you avoid paying taxes on those sales.

This is viable a rent-to-own investment strategy. A lease option investor continues to reinvest sales of their rent-to-own property into more and more rent-to-own properties, eventually becoming a serious real estate investor. A typical rental property investment is where a landlord keeps one home, gaining equity from rent and from the value of the home depending on the market. The lease option strategy is one in which the landlord is gaining properties on each sale, accumulating more and more real estate.

While it is a solid investment strategy, it is not for everyone. I personally am not interested in continuing to reinvest in rent-to-own real estate in this way so I am not going to sell our new home to pursue an opportunity like this. For me it is a question of running an ethical business, and this strategy is too much like a pyramid scheme. As someone who really had to struggle to rebuild my credit and save up for a down payment, I am far more interested in working to help people rent-to-own the right way rather than getting caught up in someone's "get rich quick" business scheme. With that said, I am a long ways away from retirement. For someone like me, but older, who has enough money to retire on and is looking for something to do after retirement, this could be a lucrative investment pathway.

However, I do not recommend it. I bring it up merely to provide you with many perspectives on buying and selling via lease option agreements. You will run into these websites and I want you to be prepared to ask the right questions to protect your investment and get as much of your money as possible. I do not have any personal experience with this type of investment so I am not offering up any advice on this except for you to make any investments in real estate very carefully. It is also important to remind you that not all rent-to-own listing services are poor choices. There are some good ones out there. Just do your homework. Remember it is all about calculated risks.

How You Sell

No matter how you have come to decide to sell you are going to need to know how to sell. Perhaps your renter has come to you and asked you to sell them the house they have been renting. You may want to jump at the chance especially if they are ready to sell right now. A rent-to-own can be a good option for you if you are not certain whether or not you want to sell. If they are serious and ready to own, they may bolt and buy a different house, so how do you keep your good renter in your home while you decide if you want to sell it? Offer them a lease option contract. Let them know that you need some time to think about it, and if they still want to buy the home after the agreed upon time frame, you will sell it to them. Offer to lock in a price right now. If you are in a good market you may lose a few dollars but it will give them some incentive so stick it out for another year as they could end up getting a much better deal out of it. And, even if you do lose a few thousand in equity on the sale, you will gain another entire year in rental equity and maintenance savings which will likely outweigh what you lose on the purchase price of the house anyway.

I recently sat next to a fellow baseball fan at a Seattle Mariners game who I overheard telling his friend that he still owns a house in Tacoma that he bought at the top of the bubble. He was saying that he can't sell it at a $50,000+ loss, so he'd rather hold onto it until it gains enough value back that he can afford to absorb the loss. He mentioned that it has gained very little in value since the downturn in the housing market and that he suspects it will again reach that value but not any time in the near future. Having been so immersed in lease options with our home purchase and writing this book I offered up a lease option sale as advice to him. He had not considered a rent-to-own but was very intrigued by the idea that two to three years of rental equity alone more than made up for the hit that he took during the downturn. He could sell the home for what it is worth now, giving the renter a chance to gain some equity on her purchase while her rental payments are steadily eliminating his equity losses. Lease options can be a win-win for sellers and buyers in a number of scenarios if they solve a problem for both sides.

You can offer to set them up with an overpay which goes into a savings which is earmarked to be a part of their down payment if not the whole thing. Watching that down payment build over the course of the next few years could be the motivation you need to decide to sell your home.

You can set a payment process up with an escrow company even if you are not facing foreclosure. It will cost you a fee, but it is managed professionally which has a lot of value. If you use that escrow company at closing they will already have a relationship with the parties in the sale. This would have helped us a lot as we did not have a real estate agent to communicate back and forth or mediate for us at closing. There were two times in which this created confusion that blew up our closing. This caused a lot of stress for all parties. If the escrow company would have understood our situation better we could have avoided this and closed months earlier.

Find a legal service and advice on preparing a rent-to-own contract (or see resources at Rent2Own-Book.com), and make sure to cover all the above bases. If you feel like you need a real estate lawyer, then have them draw up the contract. It will cost you a bit more but if you feel it protects you and your investment, then it is worth it. It is likely that you will have to do this as renters will be wary of spending the extra money for a lawyer.

If you decide to sell your home via a lease option, you will find buyers. They are out there and in my experience it is more difficult to find sellers willing to weigh all of their options and sell via rentto-own than it is to find those who are eager to try a lease option. It seems easier and safer to simply follow convention and sell on the open market. Before going with the flow, you could miss out on an opportunity to help yourself and someone else. Often those who have the courage to buck convention and do what seems counter-intuitive find the greatest rewards. By simply exploring becoming a lease option seller, you might find a great investment or save your financial future.

Chapter Checklist:
___If you are facing foreclosure do not give up. Explore all of your options including selling your home via lease option.
___Receive a non-refundable option money down payment that can be used to cover back payments owed to the bank.
___Offer a 30 month lease with a six month grace period if the renter has started the process of getting financed for their purchase but has not closed at exactly 30 months (a potential total of three years).
___Also consider an open-ended lease if you are serious

about selling.

___Be honest with your renter. Tell them everything you know about the home. Their inspector will find it anyway and you will look dishonest.

___Work with the renter to set up a payment/savings system. You can use an escrow or note servicing company for this.

___You should draw up the contract or work jointly with the buyer on language that protects both of your interests and ideally solves a problem for both parties.

___Remember that even if you are underwater on your mortgage, 30 to 36 months of rental equity can help to make up the difference before you sell.

___Try to avoid using rent-to-own web-based listing services if they take any of the money from your sale before you actually sell the home. If they take money up front, they have little interest in what happens next.

___Also be wary of any service that limits the audience to those who pay a fee-to-see as they are limiting your ability to sell you home, and are likely going to try to get money out of you up front as well.

___If you use a listing service, make sure their listings are exclusive, otherwise it should be free for you (what are you paying for if it is not exclusive?).

___If you use a listing service make sure they do not take your option payment as their "fee". You should receive a 3% option payment if you sell your home through a lease option.

> "None of us got here solely by picking ourselves up by our bootstraps. We got here because somebody - a parent, a teacher, an ivy league crony or a few nuns - bent down and helped us pick up our boots."

> Thurgood Marshall

FINDING THE AMERICAN DREAM

This rent-to-own purchase has changed our lives. We are in a completely different situation now than we were the day before we signed our paperwork to close the deal. It has been the best investment decision that either of us have ever made, including our college educations. There were two key pieces to completing our journey to home ownership and closing the deal. The first is what we learned about how to properly close a rent-to-own deal, and the other is what we discovered about the American dream.

How to close the deal: The takeaway:

To close a successful rent-to-own deal, both parties have to find common ground. Maybe that sounds obvious to you, but there is more to it than simply making it beneficial for both sides. That common ground has to be rooted in actually solving a problem for both sides. If you are confident that you and the seller are helping each other solve a problem by way of your rent-to-own purchase, then you will be far more likely to close the deal and become a homeowner. A financial arrangement that benefits both sides is crucial, but it is really only impactful if it solves a problem for both sides. If you or the seller are only in it to try to make a quick dollar, then you are setting yourself up for a rocky road. It's not impossible, but you're much less likely to succeed.

Imagine if our seller was only trying to make money on a home that he lost value in during the downturn. How could he have known that two years later the home would have gained such unprecedented equity? He could not have. If his only motivation was to make money, he would have been looking to cash in with someone else rather than honor the deal he made with us. Even though the deal would still have been mutually beneficial to both parities, the reality of the equity gains on his property would have been impossible to ignore. Rather, if he were only trying to make money, it may have appeared to him that the rent-to-own agreement itself had now become a problem.

Account for this up front. Identify the problem that is being solved for both sides. Let the sellers know that they are helping you solve a problem as well. If they only seem interested in making money off of you, be very careful because this is not the best basis for a two to three year relationship. Calculated risks and problem solving. Make this your mantra and apply it to everything as you go.

Our Discovery

What we found in our journey to find our rent-to-own home is that we ended up achieving our own little piece of the American dream. We learned that the American dream is not dead, rather people have forgotten that the American dream is one of family, co-workers, community, and nation working together. It is the story of the hard work of many and how that connects to your own personal work ethic and drive. It is an interconnected web of people who love, care and work as hard as they can every day to live and provide a better life for the next generation.

I am thankful that I didn't get to this point in life and think that it was somehow because of my own efforts only. I did not convince myself that somehow I picked myself up by the bootstraps and made it. I don't assume that I simply worked harder or was a little smarter than the others around me who are striving for the same dream. I am thankful for these things because that selfishness would seem ugly to those who helped me. Why would they ever want to help me or anyone else again if I simply forgot how hard they worked for us? That forgetting is where the American dream begins to break down. We need each other to make it happen and we must remember that.

How could I honestly ever replicate this success if I forgot what made it possible? Chances are I would begin to feel like a failure as those I need would not be there to help me the next time around. I would be looking around for those magic bootstraps that simply do not exist.

It is true that nobody picks themselves up by their bootstraps. If you believe this you have been duped. My wife had a talented high school English teacher who used to say, "A metaphor doesn't work if it doesn't work on the literal level." The idea that people can "pick themselves up by their bootstraps" is one such unworkable metaphor. Try it out for yourself. Go put on a pair of boots. The bootstraps are the loops on the back. Now try to pick yourself up just by tugging on those straps on your boots. Don't cheat and lean or sit on anything; just try and use your bootstraps to raise yourself up. Can't do it, can you? It's literally impossible to pick yourself up by your bootstraps. Why let an unworkable metaphor rule your life? It's better to admit that we all get to where we are in life by cooperating with others, and that we all have a role to play in another's success.

No matter who you are, there are hundreds, thousands, and even millions of people you have to thank for helping you. I have yet to meet anyone in the United States who can honestly say they alone are responsible for their own success. It is impossible. There are too many hard working people out there for you to claim that you did it on your own. It is almost silly to think that anyone could be totally responsible for their own success. It is almost as silly as that bootstrap metaphor.

At some point someone built a road, another built a hospital, and someone else worked as hard as they could to get through medical school. In medical school, other people helped them learn how to care for people in need. That person became a doctor, which is really hard to do, and made certain that you were safely delivered into the world. Right from the start, when you were on your way to the hospital, you were benefiting from the hard work of lots of other people.

That reliance on others does not stop after infancy. It goes on and on throughout life. It is how we came up with the idea of the American dream at all. We need each other. We cannot do it alone. I believe part of the death of the American dream for so many people is this idea that somehow we can simply pick ourselves up by our bootstraps to have a better life. It is like a great forgetting in our culture. When we say we did it by our bootstraps, we forget to honor and respect those who help us in life and by doing so we are helping to break down the American dream. We have to learn to appreciate that we need the help of others.

Without parents, many of us would not have made it but a few hours in this world. Without the thankless work of teachers, we wouldn't learn enough to survive adulthood. Without farmers many of us would starve. Farmers are some of the hardest workers alive. They work from sun up to sun down day after day. They fight like heck to raise crops and bring home a harvest, but even they can't do it alone. They need help from engineers who design efficient farm machines, scientists who develop ways to protect crops, and people who pick crops and get them into stores and eventually into your kitchen. Even with strapped boots, nobody, not even a farmer, can do that all of that by themselves.

I could go on and on. You need the help of all of us. Without all of our handwork and effort our country's economy would grind to a halt, making it difficult for anyone to achieve a good life. Everyone of us is necessary to create and sustain the American dream both for ourselves and for others. What makes it so special is that it is even possible at all. In a country the size of ours with a diverse population well over 300 million people, how we could organize ourselves in a way that works for so many is amazing, and when we all remember what it takes to achieve the American dream and act upon it, it will only get better from here.

Do your part. Remember that someone else's American dream depends on your hard work and effort. You are an important cog in someone's wheel just as someone who might be a perfect stranger right now will be your hero someday. Your work could have ripple effects for generations as well. Help people solve problems by sharing your talents and skills with people in need. Others have shared theirs with you even if you forget or do not realize it. Forget those bootstraps; almost nobody knows what they are anyway.

If getting your rent-to-own home is part of achieving your personal American dream, reflect on who you will need to help to get you there. Reflect on all of the people whose hard work has helped you already. Recognize that you will have to be willing to work every bit as hard as them to get noticed and be willing to help others along the way. Also remember to allow others to help you get there, and when you do finally arrive at your destination, thank them. Offer to help them move further down the path to their American dream too. It is the only way we can all get there. Work hard, take calculated risks, help others solve problems, and don't forget that you need their help too.

Now you are prepared. You know what you have to do. I hope writing my story helps you find your dream home. Good luck.

ABOUT THE AUTHOR

John Boyle has been studying cities and population demographics since he was 14 years old. He found an outlet for this passion at the University of Florida where he graduated Cum Laude with a degree in Political Science, City Planning and Business Geography.

He has always been an unconventional person, following his heart and chasing happiness rather than keeping up with the Joneses and chasing carrots.

John is a leader, an eternal optimist, a problem solver and a long distance runner. Visit his running blog, runjohnboyle.com, to see his favorite Seattle runs.